Connected Riding®

An Introduction

by Peggy Cummings
with Diana Deterding

Illustrations by Nancy Camp

CONNECTED RIDING, AN INTRODUCTION
by Peggy Cummings with Diana Deterding

DISCLAIMER OF LIABILITY
The author and publisher shall have neither liability nor responsibility to any person or entity with respect to any loss or damage caused or alleged to be caused directly or indirectly by the information contained in this book. While the book is as accurate as the author can make it, there may be errors, omissions, and inaccuracies.

PRIMEDIA Equine Group
656 Quince Orchard Road, #600
Gaithersburg, MD 20878

Library of Congress Catalog Card Number: 99-62974
ISBN: 0-9611314-9-7

Book and cover design by Lauryl Suire Eddlemon
Cover photography by Kathleen Wattle/Captive Spirit

To Skipper and King who sparked my passion and
Dr. James Jealous D.O. who taught me the
importance of learning from
the inside to the outside.

For their contributions to this book, I'd like to thank:

Susan Cook for her support, encouragement and friendship; Diana Deterding for her insight, enthusiasm and ability to communicate the work; Kellie Hale for introducing me to Diana; Nancy Camp for her illustrations and deep interest in the work; and Diane Cook for her able editing. I would also like to acknowledge Jan Stark, who helped me begin the process of writing; Kris McCormack, an avid student and supporter; Nikky Stinchcombe, Sherry Alexander, Dana Light, Diane Sept, Anita Imms, and Deborah Bowerman Davies, students and instructors, for their opinions and quick responses in time of need.

Connection

What am I seeking from my horse?
Is it freedom? Is it unity?
Or perhaps an undiscovered understanding?
I know the answer lies within
and when it makes itself known
it will be mine and his and ours alone.

Peggy Cummings from the poem
"The Horse Is A Mirror To My Soul"

Contents

SAFETY DISCLAIMER: The author and publisher wish to remind the reader that horseback riding and horse-related activities are by their nature hazardous and can result in serious injuries because of a variety of related and/or unrelated reasons including, but not limited to, the fact that behavior—whether of people or horses—can be unpredictable. The reader is strongly encouraged and advised to assume responsibility for her or his own actions and personal safety by complying with all standard and other sensible equine safety procedures. Please, protect yourself by wearing a properly fitted and secured certified ASTM-SEI protective equestrian helmet and appropriate riding shoes with heel when you are riding or working with horses. At all times use your best sense and consideration when around horses and other riders. This book cannot replace the reader's own sound judgement and good decision making nor can it disclose all of the potential hazards and/or risks the reader may encounter.

The material contained in this book has worked to the benefit of the author and her students. The sharing of this information is not a guarantee or promise of any results which you may or may not obtain. Although believing that her advice is sound and well-founded, the author specifically states that neither she nor the publisher will be liable to anyone for damages caused by the reader's reliance upon any of the information contained in this book.

PREFACE

Popping the last bite of breakfast in her mouth, the little girl jumped up from the table and kissed her mother good-bye. "Come on, Papi" she said, tugging on her father's hand. "It's time to go." Her mother just smiled.

It was the same every Sunday. As soon as breakfast was finished, her daughter was ready to rush off to La Fincona, a coffee plantation outside San Salvador where her husband played cricket each week. Sometimes she tried to delay their departure, but this morning she just set the paper aside with a sigh and followed them outside. "Have a good match," she told her husband. "And you," she said, bending down for a hug, "be careful and be good."

The little girl watched as her mother waved good-bye. Then settling in for the 15-mile drive, she curled up in the back seat and closed her eyes. In the stillness, she imagined the soft sounds and sweet smells that waited for her. "Soon," she whispered to herself. "We'll be there soon."

When she felt the smooth pavement of the highway turn to bumpy road, she knew they were there. As the car stopped, she jumped out with barely a word. Ducking through a stand of trees, she paused. There at the end of the plantation road was the object of her excitement—the sprawling stables of La Fincona.

Like so many little girls her age, Peggy Cummings was in love with horses. On Sunday mornings at the plantation, she spent hours brushing their manes and tails and whispering stories in their ears. She knew each of the horses by name. Knew their faces and where they liked to be rubbed. She even knew which ones liked it when she sneaked in a pair of scissors to give them a haircut. Other little girls could play with toys. For Peggy, it was horses.

By the time she was 10, the owner of the plantation had given Peggy a pony of her own. Sunday mornings were still spent at the plantation, but now she was allowed to go riding. Sometimes she visited other plantations and rode with friends, exploring coconut groves and cotton fields or splashing along the ocean beach. Life was idyllic.

Eventually, though, things began to change. By the late 1950s the political climate in El Salvador had worsened. To protect the family, her English father and American mother decided it was time to leave. With more than 18 years of distinguished service at the American embassy, Peggy's mother was in a good position to ask for a post in Washington, D.C. When it was granted, Peggy's parents were relieved, but Peggy was devastated. At 14, she would have to leave her home, her friends and the horses she loved.

Her parents knew the transition would be difficult for Peggy. To help her through it, they told her she could have her pick of schools in New England. In those days, it was customary for the children of diplomats to attend private school, so that's where Peggy concentrated her search. After being accepted by several, she selected the one with the best equestrian program—Oak Grove in Vassalboro, Maine.

Peggy didn't know it then, but the years at school in Maine would set the course for her life. Not only did her equestrian education begin in earnest, but she met the man who would instill in her a dedication to horses as well as a love of teaching. His name was "Skipper" Bartlett.

An ex-Cavalry officer, Bartlett ran the school's equestrian program with precision. Students were evaluated on their achievements and skill, and in Bartlett's mind, Peggy was lacking in both. This came as quite a shock to her. In El Salvador, Peggy had taken 10 lessons at the polo club. This, she believed, made her a good rider. Bartlett soon dispelled that notion, placing Peggy at the bottom of the class. For some, this would have been too much to take. But instead of being discouraged, Peggy worked harder. From that time on, Bartlett knew there was something special about that girl and horses.

Later that year his instincts were confirmed. When she first started school, Peggy fell in love with a 5-year-old gelding named King. The horse was so tough to handle, only one older girl was allowed to ride him. That didn't matter to Peggy. She spent every spare minute in his stall, taking care of him and learning what made him tick.

In time Peggy was allowed to ride King, but his temperament was still challenging. One afternoon Bartlett pulled Peggy aside and said he knew she was attached to the horse but unless King could be trained to let beginners ride him, he would have to go. For the next several months, Peggy spent hours with King, grooming him, touching him, working him and helping him accept people. King improved, Bartlett was impressed and allowed the horse to stay.

When summer came around, Bartlett invited Peggy to work with him at his summer riding school, to which kids from surrounding camps came for lessons. Peggy couldn't have been happier. Through long days and weeks, she helped get 14 horses ready for the onslaught of camp kids. The experience proved to be very educational.

Peggy worked summer camps with Bartlett for the next four years. The summer after Peggy's first year in college, a friend of Skipper's who ran the Tripp Lake Camp lost his assistant to a broken leg. Bartlett sent Peggy over to help out. Within a year she was heading up the riding program, a job that lasted 12 years.

During this time, Peggy's equine education continued. She learned how to select horses that could stand up to the strenuous camp days. She discovered that if you prepared horses well with groundwork and conditioning, they could work long hours with different bodies on them and still keep a good attitude. And her knowledge about the individuality of horses and people grew.

Going from one horse to the next at Tripp Lake Camp, she discovered unique combinations of personality, physical construction and talent. Every horse was different—some outgoing, some athletic, some cantankerous. From one she learned that if a child pulled on his mouth, the horse would be ready to quit by the third week of camp. Another horse, who wasn't kicked and pulled on, could be ridden five hours a day all summer long without becoming sore. All of them taught her that proper maintenance—regularly scheduled worming and shoeing, good dental care and the use of the right equipment—helped to insure a good attitude and willingness to work. They were lessons Peggy would never forget.

During the camp years, Peggy married, had six children, earned a Horsemaster's Certificate from Potomac Horse Center, and began her own training program. But when her twins were born in 1977, the challenge of juggling kids, camp and barn finally became too great. She gave up the camp and settled into teaching and holding clinics at home. The next phase of her education had begun.

Always hungry for knowledge, Peggy invited some of the most innovative clinicians of the time to her barn in Maine. H.L.M. Van Shaik, Lendon Gray and others contributed to her riding skills. But eventually even the best trainers were unable to help Peggy progress. Frustrated and depressed, she finally had to admit that she could go no further—not because of lack of talent or desire, but because of pain and discomfort.

Like so many riders, Peggy discovered, as she moved into her 40s, that the years of traditional riding had taken their toll on her body. Her back was in constant pain and her legs were beginning to protest her daily riding routine. If something didn't happen soon, Peggy would have to seriously curtail her riding.

It was time to refocus her efforts. Now, instead of trying to find ways to improve her riding skills, she began looking for ways to recapture the joy and ease of riding she had known as a child. First she found Sally Swift, of *Centered Riding*™ fame, who taught her about body work and learning how to ride pain-free. Then, Linda Tellington-Jones, originator of TTEAM™, added to her knowledge of the whole-horse-and-rider concept. Finally,

Major Andres Lindgren taught her exercises to take care of issues with the horse. All three helped Peggy move in the right direction.

In the end, Peggy developed a unique riding and training method that blended what she had learned from people with what she had learned from horses themselves. She conquered her own pain and, for the first time as an adult, rode with complete freedom—just as she had at La Fincona.

Today Peggy shares what she's learned over a lifetime through a riding and training approach called *Connected Riding*®. Leaving her home in Idaho for nine months out of the year, she travels across the country giving demonstrations, clinics and seminars. She also holds seminars for instructors to teach them how to help their students gain an awareness of biomechanical and mental techniques that allow them to move in harmony with the horse. It's an all-consuming job that's taken the passion of a little girl and turned it into a mission for the grown woman.

Peggy's hope is that eventually the rigid, traditional ways of teaching riding will give way to the flowing, natural movement taught through *Connected Riding*®. She knows it will take considerable work, but she's making headway.

In front of a packed lecture hall in Louisville, Kentucky, she asks, "Who wants to learn how to dance?" As hands raise one by one, she can't help but smile. "All right then, let's begin."

Introduction

As I travel around the country, the first thing people ask me is, "What is *Connected Riding*®?" It sounds interesting, this concept of "connection," but with so many training methods being taught today, what makes this one different?

Connected Riding® is fundamentally different from the traditional riding approaches most of you have encountered in the past. It teaches you how to ride from the inside (by feeling), to the outside (by action). It provides you with an awareness of body and movement that empowers you to move in harmony with the horse. It's connection—and ultimately that's what all of us are striving for—a connection that allows us to perform better, communicate better and have a personal relationship with our horses.

As you explore *Connected Riding*®, you'll find that it will challenge some of the basic principles you've learned about riding—especially in terms of position and aids. It will ask you to learn about your own body and how it moves. It will ask you to become self-reliant and understanding. It will ask you to become a student of the horse—not just a student of riding. And, finally, it will ask you to take responsibility for leading the dance that connection creates.

It sounds like a lot to accomplish. And it is. But even though it will take awareness, work and maybe even a little frustration, I promise you this: If you're up to the challenge, the rewards are tremendous. You'll never be more exhilarated than the first time you move in perfect harmony with your horse. Nothing is more beautiful than the graceful rhythm you'll feel as your horse flows freely beneath you. Nothing is more rewarding than a true partnership based on understanding, friendship and cooperation.

I've had the opportunity to help thousands of riders from all walks of life and every riding discipline begin the journey of *Connected Riding*®. All of them have discovered something new about themselves, their horses and their lives.

They've also helped me discover that all bodies, both human and horse, have something that blocks the freedom to move; be it the mind —"I don't know how to do that!"—or body. Even when someone comes to me with very real physical problems such as a fused spine, uneven legs, or limbs repaired with pins, it doesn't matter. When people are taught to respond to a situation with the intent to move rather than stiffen, even the most limited bodies— horse and rider—find more comfort, freedom and joy. Every human and horse with whom I've worked have found their own potential for movement. It's my hope that this book will begin to do the same for you.

We'll start by refreshing some basics on equine movement to allow us to understand better what we ask our horses to do. Then we'll take a look at the kind of riders we are today and discover the kind of riders we can be. Next, we'll begin the exploration of our own body awareness and finally, we'll put what we've learned to use in the saddle.

I suggest you read the entire book through before you begin the exercises. Then go back and do the work at a pace that's comfortable for you and your horse. The nice thing about a book is that there's no time limit—no end of class or clinic to rush you. You must take your time and let the principles of *Connected Riding*® become a part of you.

If you're currently in training, pay particular attention to the final chapter. It contains "translations" of what your trainer is asking for and how to apply *Connected Riding®* techniques to those instructions. Many of my students have had extensive training and find they can easily incorporate *Connected Riding®* into their performance with great success once they've mastered awareness of their bodies.

Some, however, do find their trainers a little resistant to having new ideas interjected into their established training methods. If that happens, you'll need to make some decisions. Just let me say this—I'm here to support trainers, not undermine them. *Connected Riding®* has helped hundreds of trainers enable their students to interpret instruction better and perform more freely and effectively—regardless of discipline. After all, what we're talking about here is human body movement being connected to horse body movement in one harmonious dance. Different disciplines are just different dances with riders and horses wearing different costumes.

If you're a new rider, that's great. You have an opportunity to begin your relationship with your horse in a balanced, connected way. Without all the old habits to undo, you'll find it much easier to find the flow and rhythm of the dance. Just remember—whether you're a beginner or an accomplished rider—take your time. There's no time limit on success. It will wait for you at the end of the road.

Peggy Cummings

Chapter 1

Motion is the Means

"And God took the West Wind and
created the horse . . ."
The Koran

When I first began riding horses as a child in El Salvador, I did-n't think about how a horse was built or what he did to create this or that movement. All I cared about was climbing on his back.

When I look back on that time now, I realize that it was the purest riding I have ever done. Unhampered by instructions to sit up straight, hold my hands just so, and all the other restrictive messages we give each other, my horse and I just let nature take over. My body moved with his rhythm and he responded to my direction without thinking. We were connected.

As I grew older and formalized my riding, I began to lose some of that natural connection. The frustrating part was, I didn't know why. I spent countless hours and dollars on lessons, books, clinics, seminars and videos trying to find my way back. From this one, I would learn one piece. From that one, another piece, but I still wasn't able to recapture the connection I had as a child.

Finally I found the answer in horses themselves. To get con-nected, I needed to give back to the horse his ability to move as nature intended. Not crammed up, jammed up or held in, but

13

relaxed and in balance. This understanding is really where my journey to connection began. And why we start with movement here.

Body Basics

A horse's body is a complex structure containing about 205 bones (**Figure 1-1**) held together and animated by muscles, joints, tendons and ligaments. Every horse, regardless of breed or size, is built essentially the same. The length and angle of bones may vary from breed to breed, but each uses his parts to move in a way unique to the horse.

As students of riding, we'll be concerned primarily with the body elements that affect movement—joints and muscle groups. I recommend that at some point you take the time to acquaint yourself fully with equine anatomy, but for now, this fundamental knowledge will help you understand what makes a horse move so you can move with him.

JOINTS

One of the most fundamental concepts of *Connected Riding®* is this: All skeletal

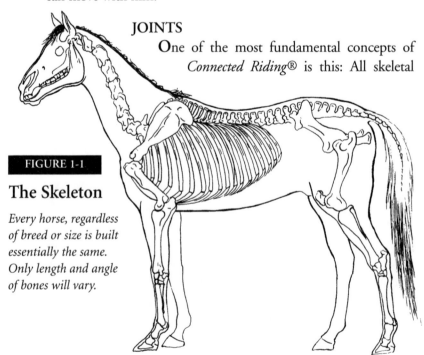

FIGURE 1-1

The Skeleton

Every horse, regardless of breed or size is built essentially the same. Only length and angle of bones will vary.

creatures are capable of movement because of joints. If joints are restricted, movement is hampered or stopped. It's as simple as that. Joints that are free create movement. Joints that are restricted stop movement.

A good way to visualize this concept is to imagine the horse as a marionette. Every bone is like a lever and every joint is like a hinge that connects one part of the horse to the next. That being the case, what would happen if an invisible hand reached out and applied pressure to a pivotal hinge? What happens to the hinges above and below it?

That's right. Not much.

If one hinge is restricted, the free flow of movement is interrupted. Often in our riding we restrict the movement of the joints, resulting in a loss of motion and natural carriage. To avoid this, we need to know which "hinge" does what and how it works to keep everything flowing smoothly. **Tables 1-1-3** and **Figures 1-2-3** provide a breakdown of the most important joints with the type of movement each promotes. As we progress through *Connected Riding*®, you can refer to these charts to understand better what you're asking your horse to do and how you might be inhibiting his ability to do it.

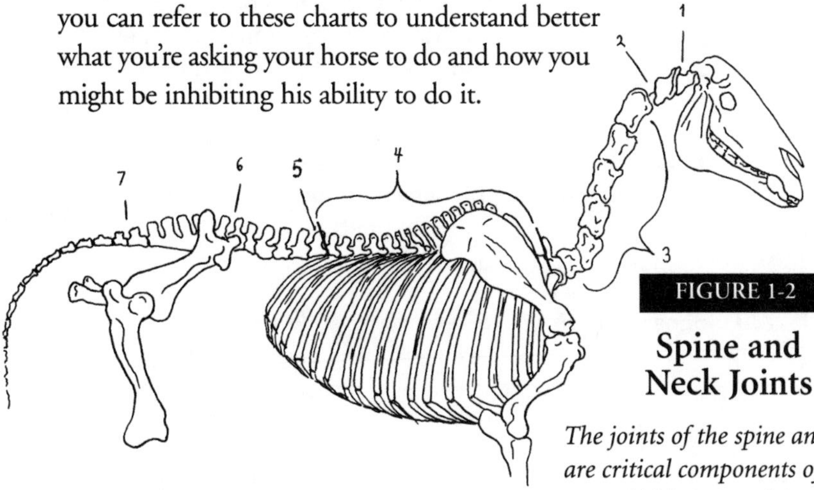

FIGURE 1-2

Spine and Neck Joints

The joints of the spine and neck are critical components of movement. Table 1-1 explains the function of the important joints.

TABLE 1-1

These are the key "hinges" in your horse's topline.

Axial Skeleton Joints	Movement
1. Poll Joint	Allows flexion and extension of the head at the first cervical vertebra. This joint is key to the horse's balance and response to the bridle.
2. Axis Joint	This joint, found between the first and second vertebrae, permits the head to flex from side to side. This is where true rotation of the poll takes place.
3. Cervical Vertebrae	The remaining cervical vertebrae allow up and down and side-to-side flexion and extension of the neck.
4. Ribs	They can flex up and down with a slight rotation during breathing. The flexibility of the long, thin rib bones and the intercostal cartilage makes this possible.
5. Thoracic Lumbar Junction	This area maintains flexibility when the horse is using his abdominals and major muscles of the hind-quarters for impulsion.
6. Lumbosacral Joint	A key joint, it allows the horse to flex the loin and bring the hind leg forward–for movement and balance.
7. Coccygeal Joints	Allow very free movement up, down and sideways; they reflect the position and tension or relaxation of the back.

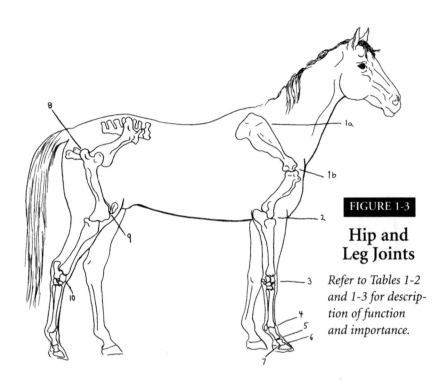

FIGURE 1-3

Hip and Leg Joints

Refer to Tables 1-2 and 1-3 for description of function and importance.

MUSCLES

If joints are the hinges of the marionette, muscles are the elastic strings that move the hinges. Layered throughout the body, muscles function by contracting and relaxing, causing movement of bones. The muscles are attached to bones by tendons; when one group of muscle bends or flexes a joint, an opposing group extends or straightens it in a reciprocal manner.

In an ideal athlete, muscles work in harmony, contracting and relaxing in a regular rhythm. No muscle or muscle group is overworked or underworked, and all develop evenly and remain fit. This is important because muscle development and fitness affect a horse's balance, strength, stamina and agility—especially when he's being ridden. If a muscle is weak, it's harder for it to influence its adjoining part into motion. The more effort it takes, the more energy is burned and the quicker the muscles and the horse tire.

The following table show joints that affect the motion of the legs.

Foreleg Joints	Movement
1a. Shoulder Sling	The shoulders are not joined to the trunk by a bony joint but by a "sling" of muscles. They glide freely over the ribs and rotate forward and backward. The shoulders can tilt sideways to reach outward with the whole foreleg or to bring the foreleg inward for lateral movement.
1b. Shoulder Joint	Flexion and extension at this joint is mostly forward and backward, moving the whole foreleg. Lateral movement is limited.
2. Elbow Joint	The elbow flexes and extends forward and backward only.
3. Knee Joint	The joint is made up of seven bones between the forearm (radius), and cannon and splint bones (metacarpal bones). It only flexes forward and backward.
4. Fetlock Joint	Flexes only forward and backward. It also serves as a shock absorber by allowing the pastern to sink under the weight of the horse. The same action is present in the hind leg.

(continued)

Foreleg Joints	Movement
5. Pastern Joint	What little movement this joint has is mostly forward and backward. The same action is present in the hind leg.
6. Coffin Joint	What little movement this joint has is mostly forward and backward. The same action is present in the hind leg.
7. Navicular Joint	Allows little movement, but cushions the deep digital flexor tendon, which passes over the navicular bone and attaches to the underside of the coffin bone; it absorbs shock at each stride. The same action is present in the hind leg.

Hind Leg Joints	Movement
8. Hip Joint	A ball and socket joint that moves forward and backward. Some lateral movement is also possible. It moves the whole hind leg.
9. Stifle Joint	Between the thigh bone and the kneecap, it moves forward and backward.
10. Hock Joint	Made up of six bones between the tibia and the cannon and splint bones. It flexes only forward and backward. The hock and stifle are reciprocal joints; that is, when one flexes or extends, the other must do the same.

One of the things that affect muscle development is uneven use. So when you're reminded to work a horse consistently and on both sides, be sure to listen. Another is compression in the spine— of either horse or rider. To help your horse develop and use his muscles naturally, it's best to avoid the use of restrictive equipment such as martingales, draw reins, side reins, spurs and other gimmicks that cause compression of the horse's spine. You also need to minimize restriction from the rider. Tightness of the rider's spine, clamping of both legs together, riding behind the vertical, pushing with the seat, leaning, sitting on only one seat bone, or any other type of compression affects the muscle use of the horse. In short, any method of working a horse in restriction or with compression affects the whole system and should be avoided. But that's what *Connected Riding®* is all about. So as we progress through the book, you'll learn how to help your horse move and develop his muscles naturally.

To help evaluate the muscle fitness of your horse, consider these questions:

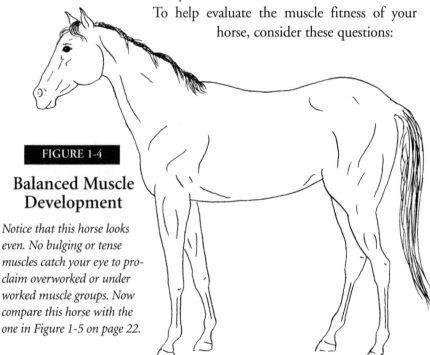

FIGURE 1-4

Balanced Muscle Development

Notice that this horse looks even. No bulging or tense muscles catch your eye to proclaim overworked or under worked muscle groups. Now compare this horse with the one in Figure 1-5 on page 22.

- *Does your horse move more freely at liberty than he does when being ridden?*
- *Do his veins "pop" soon after work begins?*
- *Does he sweat profusely every time you ride, despite the weather?*
- *Is he overmuscled or undermuscled?*
- *Is he uneven in his movement or his appearance?*

Check to see if your horse is balanced and fit as in **Figure 1-4** or uneven like the horse in **Figure 1-5**. Remember, muscles are kept in optimum condition by use, proper exercise, nutrition, balanced shoeing and *Connected Riding*®. A regular routine of muscle toning and maintenance should be a part of your horse care program, especially if you and your horse compete.

The Elements of Movement

Now that we've taken a very basic look at what enables a horse to move, let's look at how he actually does it. While the marionette was a good example of the anatomy of movement, the old rear-engined VW Beetle is a good example of a horse's power in movement. The experts agree that revving up this power while controlling it with our bodies is an important part of riding. What they can't always agree on, however, is just how to do it. I used to join the debates, until I realized the answer is really pretty simple—let the horse move in as close to riderless form as possible. If we do, we can capture the forces of motion and move ahead. If we don't, we create a reaction against the forces and make forward movement more difficult—just as we would if we blocked the forward movement of the Beetle by not engaging the clutch.

So how do we capture the natural forces of motion? As you can see from **Figure 1-6**, motion begins behind and moves forward through the body. When a horse is moving freely, he releases his poll, the withers release and the shoulders free up. This action brings the back up, allowing the horse to use his hindquarters to propel

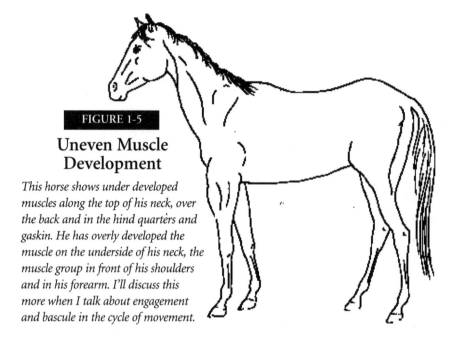

FIGURE 1-5

Uneven Muscle Development

This horse shows under developed muscles along the top of his neck, over the back and in the hind quarters and gaskin. He has overly developed the muscle on the underside of his neck, the muscle group in front of his shoulders and in his forearm. I'll discuss this more when I talk about engagement and bascule in the cycle of movement.

himself forward. It's the active use of his hindquarters coming through to the front, or engagement, that gives the horse his power—and it's the act of engagement that we look for when we ride.

ENGAGEMENT

"Engage the hindquarters" is something most riders misconstrue. In simplest terms, engagement is the act of bringing the hind leg forward under the body to provide the thrust needed for impulsion. (Compare **Figures 1-6** and **1-7**.) During true engagement, the back lifts, the neck and poll are released, and the topline of the horse becomes rounded. To achieve this, the croup is lowered with an increased flexion in the hind limb joints. The farther the hind leg reaches, the longer the stride and the greater the pushing power.

Most riders we see today, even at the highest levels, rarely achieve true engagement. The primary reason for this is either a rider position that promotes compression rather than expansion or a jammed spine in the horse. It's a bit like a Slinky® toy going down the stairs. If it's new it moves smoothly along. But if there's a kink in it, it stops. Watch your horse at liberty to see how he engages naturally. If he comes under himself well when free, chances are you're the kink in the Slinky®. If he's stuck, I incorporate *Connected®* groundwork exercises in his routine to help unstick him.

BASCULE

Another important concept of movement is bascule, a French word that means "an arch that comes into being through movement." It happens when a horse is in flight over a jump or when he moves in true collection, giving him poise, balance and an elastic back mechanism.

Of course, a horse must be able to bascule (arch) and flex (bend) through turns as well. This rounding takes place primarily in the lumbosacral joint and ***can only happen when the back muscles are relaxed.*** When back muscles are tense or contracted, the back will hollow and the belly will drop, resulting in stiff movement and compromised balance. This condition puts the horse on the forehand and creates a false frame. So, when your instructor is asking you to "lighten up" your horse, what she

FIGURE 1-6

The Cycle of Movement

Showing Engagement and Bascule

It is important that a horse release his base by lowering the poll, raising the wither and bringing the legs under, in order to travel forward with impulsion and in balance. The poll must be released to allow the head and neck to telescope forward. When the withers release, the shoulder will swing freely and the back will come up. With a release in the lumbosacral joint, the hind quarters will engage, there will be increased bend in the joints of the hind legs and the horse will come through from behind with a longer stride.

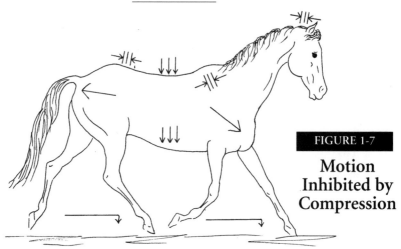

FIGURE 1-7

Motion Inhibited by Compression

At first glance this horse may appear the same as the horse in Figure 1-6, but notice that this horse is traveling on his forehand. Compression in the poll prevents the telescoping of the head and neck. The back is dropped, which inhibits the swing of the shoulder. The lumbosacral joint is jammed so the pelvis is stuck out behind and the hind legs are swinging forward with less bend in the joints, less engagement, resulting in a shorter stride.

really is asking for is bascule (releasing his base). This can't happen if you have a lot of tense weight in your hand, squeeze in your legs or push in your seat. Why? Because when your horse is restricted by you, your equipment or your position, his back muscles will be tense, stiff and restricted, making bascule and engagement impossible.

BALANCE

Balance is intimately related to bascule. Picture the last time you watched a horse running free. The sway of his neck, the lengthening stride, his power and grace. It's hypnotic. But if you look past the beauty of the moment, you might realize that he isn't just running. He is constantly readjusting his balance by moving his head up and down or shifting his weight forward or back, bending and arching as needed. This continuous adjustment of balance through movement is what allows a horse to run at great speeds, stop suddenly, maneuver around objects and carry a rider on his back. While balance depends on several things, two structural elements have a great deal of influence on a horse's ability to balance—the structure and set of the head and neck and the flexibility of the back.

THE HEAD OR NECK

Because the horse's head is a heavy weight at the end of a long, flexible neck, the size of the head and the length of the neck can greatly influence natural balance during movement. Table 1-4 shows some of the neck characteristics with which you should be familiar.

Choosing a horse that has natural balance for the activity you intend for him will make both of your lives easier. Nothing is more distressing to horse or rider than working with a partner unsuited for the dance.

THE FLEXIBLE BACK

The other element we'll look at in considering balance and connection is the horse's back. It not only carries the rider, but allows the horse to transmit power and movement from the hindquarters through the rest of the body. All motion of the limbs and neck is synthesized and processed in the back. Rhythmic, segmental contractions and reciprocal relaxation of the muscles of the back allows for a buoyant and energetic gait. Without a relaxed and elastic back,

TABLE 1-4

Neck Characteristic	Result
Well-proportioned head on a long neck	Produces a long stride because the long muscles of the neck draw the foreleg forward.
Low-set neck	Produces forward balance and moving on the forehand.
Higher set neck	Makes collection and high action easier.
Ewe neck	Is the result of a high head carriage and an inverted frame. It restricts the ability of the horse to flex at the poll.
Short, thick, heavy neck	Produces short strides and travels heavily on the forehand.

TABLE 1-5	
Back Construction	**Result**
Long back	Makes collection more difficult.
Hollow back	Is a result of inadequate collection and stiff riding. Hollow back often results in Sway back. Collection is difficult as horse cannot effectively push from the hindquarters.
Sway back	Is a result from long term hollow back. It is a permanent change. The horse cannot push from the hindquarters. Collection cannot happen.
Roach back (rounded up)	Makes it difficult for the horse to lighten the forehand.
Very short back	Inhibits springy movement.

no horse can reach his athletic potential. The ability to do this depends partly on the construction and flexibility of the back. Table 1-5 points out the relationship between the construction of the back and the horse's ability to collect.

If the primary goal of your riding is collection, a moderate length of back is best. Be sure to pay close attention to the proportions of the back when asking your horse to work for you. For all the energetic connection which can take place in a horse's back, when we place a stiff weight (human) in the middle of these rhythmic contractions, the inter-dependent motion can stop and the rhythm and buoyancy is destroyed.

As we progress in *Connected Riding*®, the principles of movement covered in this chapter will help you to understand how to complement your horse's natural movement and determine his ability to succeed at the tasks you've chosen for him.

Now let's take a look at ourselves.

26

Chapter 2

What Kind of Rider Are You?

"Know Thyself"
Socrates

After working with thousands of riders, I have found one thing is painfully clear—the way most of us were taught to hold our bodies is contrary to the way our bodies are built to move. Like horses, people have a natural way of going that is meant to keep us in balance and allow us to move without pain, resistance or awkwardness. But the postural habits in our society sometimes teach us to tilt the pelvis forward unnaturally as in "sit (or stand) up straight" while failing to teach us to "rebalance" the body from compressive postures such as slouching. Our bodies become accustomed to an alignment that supports a pelvis that is either slightly forward or slightly back most of the time. That's why we have so many backaches and other pains.

You might ask, "What does this have to do with riding?" And I would have to say, "Everything." You take your postural habits with you everywhere you go—even on a horse. In riding, the position of the pelvis is one of the most important elements of balance, freedom of movement and communication with the horse. In other words, everything flows from or is restricted by your seat.

Think again about the marionette from Chapter 1—only this time you're the marionette. Now, imagine yourself sitting in a saddle. An invisible hand moves forward and applies Super Glue to the joints that move your pelvic area. How easy is it to move your upper body? How easy is it to move your legs?

It isn't. In fact, movement is greatly restricted. And yet when we sit in a saddle with either a forward or backward tilt, it's essentially the same as gluing our seat shut. The lower spine is compressed, balancing becomes less natural, and muscles that are normally used for movement are called upon to maintain balance. Using muscles in this counterproductive way takes more effort and often creates stress, discomfort or pain in the lower back, shoulders and joints. Most of the time we're not aware this is happening. All we know is that something is wrong and our bodies hurt.

Before you can begin to correct the conditions that cause you to be out of balance or in pain, you need to identify your current riding position. This quick quiz can help you. Most riders fall into one of four categories: Arched Equitator, Pocket Sitter, Gumby or Connected Rider. After completing the quiz, refer to the answer chart to determine your riding style.

FIGURE 2-1

The Arched Equitator

The Arched Equitator is an all too common result of the "posture police" in our lives.

RIDER POSITION QUIZ

		Yes	No
1.	Do you hollow your back?	❏	❏
2.	Do you ride with a fairly straight arm?	❏	❏
3.	Does your leg go back to cue?	❏	❏
4.	Do you put weight on the stirrup to get your heels down?	❏	❏
5.	Do you clench your jaw? Do you hold your breath?	❏	❏
6.	Does your pelvic position vary from front to back?	❏	❏
7.	Do you have low back pain?	❏	❏
8.	Are your feet placed in front of your hips?	❏	❏
9.	Is it difficult to get your horse to listen to your cues?	❏	❏
10.	Do you have pain in your shoulders or discomfort between your shoulder blades?	❏	❏
11.	Do you slump or arch in different situations?	❏	❏
12.	Do you squeeze your hands or bend your wrists?	❏	❏
13.	Is your pelvis positioned back?	❏	❏
14.	Do you separate your hands to get the horse to round?	❏	❏
15.	Do you constantly lose one stirrup?	❏	❏
16.	Do your hips rock back and forth trying to absorb the horse's movement?	❏	❏
17.	Do you ride "chest up," shoulders back?	❏	❏
18.	Do you sit against the movement, especially in transitions?	❏	❏
19.	Do you slump your sternum and rib cage when you sit?	❏	❏

(continued)

	Yes	No
20. Is your pelvis positioned forward?	❑	❑
21. Do you press in stirrups, especially in transitions?	❑	❑
22. Do you have discomfort in your hips, knees or ankles?	❑	❑
23. Do you ride with long stirrups?	❑	❑
24. Do you have any muscle pain when you ride?	❑	❑

Answer Chart: The following chart will help you determine your normal riding position. Record the numbers of the questions to which you answered "Yes." Then find the rider type that contains most of your "Yes" numbers.

Rider Type–"Yes" Numbers

Arched Equitator: 1, 3, 4, 5, 7, 10, 12, 14, 15, 17, 20, 22, 24

Pocket Sitter: 2, 5, 8, 13, 18, 19, 21, 23, 24

Gumby: 6, 9, 11, 16, 24

If you answered no to more than 20 of the questions, you're probably a Connected Rider. The following descriptions of the different riding types should confirm what the quiz told you.

THE ARCHED EQUITATOR

Have you listened well when your mother, your teacher and, later, your riding instructor told you to sit up straight? If so, chances are these instructions, given over a lifetime, have become an automatic part of your posture and movement. Unfortunately, by pleasing your "mentors," you created problems for yourself. However good their intentions, the "posture police" in your life inadvertently have caused you to function primarily with a pelvis that is tilted

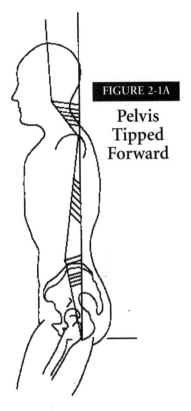

FIGURE 2-1A

Pelvis Tipped Forward

This is the pelvic position of the Arched Equitator; motion of the hip joint is limited and the upper body is more subject to being left behind the motion or thrown forward. The axis is the upper body is broken and the stress lines in the illustration indicate where a body in this position will have to use muscles to pull or hold the torso upright. This is not natural balance and requires effort that results in tension and discomfort. When mirrored by the horse he will go head high and hollow backed.

forward, causing your back to arch (hollow) and throwing your body out of alignment (**Figure 2-1-1a**). This posture is what gives this first rider its name— The Arched Equitator.

If you're not an Arched Equitator yourself, chances are you know one. This type of rider tends to bob backward instead of forward when the horse moves, ending up behind the movement. (When mirrored by the horse, he may go head high and hollow-backed as well.) In downward transitions, the hips are likely to move from side to side instead of imperceptibly forward-back. Often at the canter in certain disciplines including hunt seat and western pleasure, the seat leaves the saddle, marking time, and the upper body is slightly forward. In other disciplines like dressage, the upper body gets inclined behind the vertical to absorb the canter and sitting trot. All of this combines to cause lower back pain and discomfort between the shoulder blades, in the hips, knees and ankles. It also takes more effort to translate commands to the horse.

Also, when the pelvis is forward, the natural instinct to rebalance is lost. This is especially critical when the rider should be moving with the horse and constantly rebalancing to the horse's movements. Without this constant rebalancing, the rider becomes very heavy on the horse's back.

FIGURE 2-2

The Pocket Sitter

More common with men and often the result of spending a great deal of time at a desk.

If you recognize yourself as an Arched Equitator, you're not alone. It's a common occurrence, especially for the female rider. As we move through the *Connected Riding*® techniques you'll learn specific exercises and tips to help you relax your back and bring it into natural alignment with the rest of your body.

THE POCKET SITTER

Pocket sitting is especially prevalent in western riding and fox hunting and is more common with men whose anatomy lends itself to a backward tilt of the pelvic complex (**Figure 2-2-2a**). This type of rider exhibits the collapse of the sternum and rib cage when seated. Shoulders are rounded forward, and the head and neck jut out. People who spend a great deal of time working at a desk or doing detailed tasks are especially prone to this type of posture in everyday life and tend to bring it to the saddle.

The Pocket Sitter generally feels the effects of his posture between the shoulder blades and in the neck and arms. He normally rides with a straight arm and will tend to wear his stirrups long,

The pelvic position of the Pocket Sitter results in a "heavy" and restricted leg. Balance is unsteady. Again, the axis of the upper body is broken. The stress lines in the illustration indicate where a body in this position will have to use muscles to pull or hold the torso upright, defying natural balance and requiring effort that results in tension and discomfort. When mirrored by the horse, he will go heavy on the forehand and behind the vertical.

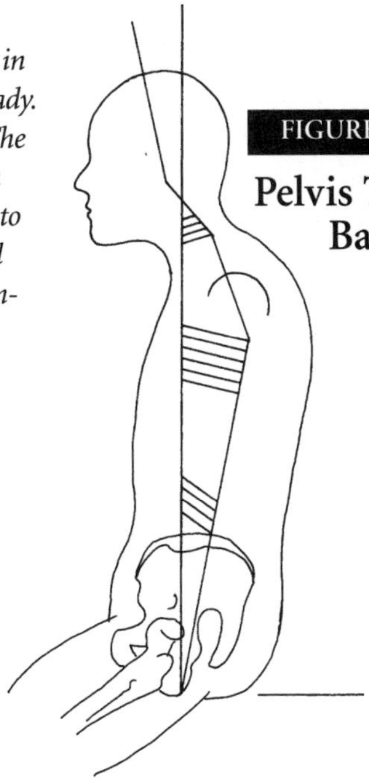

FIGURE 2-2A

Pelvis Tipped Back

causing him to tighten his toes to reach for the stirrup or keep it from sliding. This can make for some pretty tired feet at the end of a long day and will probably cause some discomfort in the thigh muscles as well.

From the horse's standpoint, this style of riding makes communication through the hands and legs difficult to achieve. It also causes the rider's leg to feel "heavy." Often, but not always, you'll see the horse mirror the posture of the rider by going heavy on the forehand and the poll and behind the vertical. If you're a Pocket Sitter, *Connected Riding*® will help you bring your body into alignment in the saddle and soften your arms and legs to increase communication with your horse.

THE GUMBY®

Some of you may realize you're sometimes an Arched Equitator and at other times a Pocket Sitter. Or maybe you just ride in "hyper" motion—always moving. If that's the case, you're probably a "Gumby"®—named after the flexible little guy in the toy store (**Figure 2-3-3a**).

This rider is more difficult to recognize than the others. If the quiz placed you in this category, you probably consider yourself fairly connected. That's not unusual. Quite often the Gumby® rider is very supple with a spine that gives in the lumbar area somewhat like

FIGURE 2-3

The Gumby®

This rider is generally all over the place and can mistake hyper-mobility for balance.

a caterpillar. But suppleness doesn't necessarily mean connected, and, without connection, the lines of communication are cut off. If you're a Gumby® rider, finding a quiet place to ride will greatly enhance your communication skills and help you when trouble arises in your riding environment. As you go through the exercises be aware of both the Arched Equitator and Pocket Sitter positions. This knowledge will help you further define your postural challenges.

THE CONNECTED RIDER

The ideal all riders should strive for is the Connected Rider (**Figure 2-4**). By riding in balance you achieve connection. This enables you to communicate better with your horse and allows you to move freely with the natural movement of the horse's body. Through connection, everyone, regardless of build or physical condition, can make riding more comfortable, effective and fun.

Throughout this book we'll talk about how you can become a Connected Rider by achieving a position of dynamic balance. Often we'll refer to this position of dynamic balance as having the pelvis in "neutral," which means an unrestricted position that

FIGURE 2-4

The Connected Rider

The ideal all riders should strive to obtain.

allows movement. **Table 2-1** outlines the results of a neutral pelvis and gives us a glimpse of what we're striving to achieve.

You might want to make a photocopy of the **Connected Rider Checklist** to have on hand as a reference as we continue.

Now that you've 1) acquainted yourself with how a horse moves; 2) gained some insight into how your particular horse is built to move; and 3) identified the type of rider you currently are, you're ready to put some of this knowledge to use.

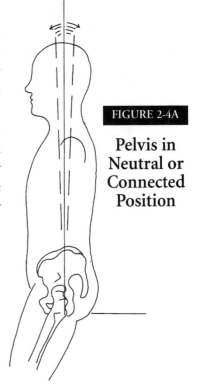

FIGURE 2-4A

Pelvis in Neutral or Connected Position

This position allows the rider to "rebalance" naturally. Notice that the axis or the upper body is unbroken and without stress or strain. The natural "rebalancing" action is a slight buoy effect. This position in riding enables the horse to release his base and travel freely.

TABLE 2-1

Checklist for the Connected Rider

Head	The head is centered over the shoulders with the chin parallel to the ground; the back of the neck and the jaw are relaxed.
Upper Torso	The upper body is free to move from the hips, allowing a buoy-like movement, which is the body's innate ability to readjust and maintain balance with the motion of the horse.
Breathing	Proper breathing using the diaphragm is an essential part of maintaining balance. Exhalation allows the body to "catch up" with the motion and rebalance itself.
Arms & Hands	The whole arm complex is soft, above the horse's withers, with the arms in a straight line from the bit to the elbow and ready to move up or down, forward or back with the movement of the horse's head.
Wrists	Wrists should always be straight, not bent in or out.
Elbows	Elbows should always remain bent, soft and flexible.
Lower Back	The lower back should be full and soft.
Seat	The seat is centered over the middle of the seat bones.
Hips	Hips are open and centered over the seat bones.
Legs	The legs hang free out of the open hip joint.
Knees	There should always be bend in the knees no matter which style of riding you use. A straight knee is an ineffective hinge.
Feet	The stirrup is placed just behind the ball of the foot, allowing the joints to move. The foot is positioned parallel to the ground.

Chapter 3

Finding the Feeling

"I hear and forget. I see and remember.
I do and understand"
Chinese Proverb

Until now, we've been talking theory. In this chapter we go beyond theory and begin to find out what it's like to be connected. It's important to understand that connection is more than a posture. It's a feeling as well. When your body is in dynamic balance and in neutral pelvis, and therefore connected, it's light, buoyant and free. A student once called it the essence of harmony, and I think that's a good description. Harmony—with your horse and with your body.

Most people find that feeling harmony for the first time is a moving experience. It's like dancing a waltz with the perfect partner—you don't want it to end. Unfortunately, it not only ends, it usually doesn't last long. The first time I was aware of the connection as an adult, I was elated. Then my mind started to analyze what I was doing, and I lost it. But it had happened, and now I knew it could be done. All I had to do was find a way to recapture it at will.

Over time I did. By breaking some ingrained habits that were keeping me from connection and by finding a cycle of rebalance that kept the connection going, I was able to bring my life and my riding into balance. Throughout this chapter we'll talk about how you can do the same for yourself.

Breaking Habits

Our culture's habit is to react to stress with compression-that is, tightening and stiffening. Most of the time, we don't even know it's happening. We just know we're tight, sore, tired or even grouchy. These feelings affect all aspects of our lives, including our riding and our horses. So, if we want to be better riders, we first have to break our cycle of how we react to stress. It will take time and focus—much like quitting smoking or resisting ice cream—but it can be done by incorporating the following five steps into your life.

Awareness

The first step to changing a habit is to be aware of it and identify it as something you want to change. Note what makes your body tighten as you go through a typical day. Do the same for a stressful day. Record them in a diary and keep track of your progress as you let go of the things that cause stress in your life.

Willingness to Release

All of us hold on to patterns of thinking that cause us stress—patterns such as, "sit up straight" or, "if I just work harder, I can do this". By identifying these thought patterns and letting go of stressful ways of thinking, you can learn other ways to accomplish the same goal in a less stressful way.

Identify the patterns in your life that cause you stress and write them in your diary. Take each pattern and look for a way to accomplish the same task or goal in a less stressful way. Every time you identify a new, stressful pattern, write it down and find an alternative. As you work on changing these patterns you'll find it easier to identify stress in your life and ways to alleviate it.

Connection

Connection is something you gain by letting go of stress and being aware of your body and your feelings. When this happens you may feel an emotional lift. There may also be physical changes as the compression of stress lets go and your body falls into its natural alignment and you become grounded. In the beginning this may seem elusive or fleeting, but don't worry. It will come and go. Once you know what it feels like, you'll be able to recapture it. We'll identify ways to do this as we progress through the chapter.

Movement

Movement keeps us dynamic instead of static. By adding the ability to respond to stress or tightness with movement, we allow ourselves to release. Unfortunately, most of us do just the opposite. We don't move through stress, we hold it in. The next time you feel tightness from stress, move your body to release it by stretching, taking a walk or even rebalancing your body where you sit or stand. It works. To help you identify the benefits of movement, record in your diary the times you used movement to reduce stress. This will help establish movement as a new and useful habit in your life.

Appreciation or "Thank you"

All of us need appreciation in our lives—including appreciation from ourselves. The final step in letting go of the stress habit is allowing yourself to notice what you've accomplished. Say "thank you" to yourself for a job well done, both mentally and in your diary. Then continue to repeat the steps you took to bring about change. Remember, it's not just bad habits that are built through repetition—good habits become a part of us in the same way. It is through repetition that you gain new awareness, more freedom, more ability to change and recapture the feeling of movement.

Groundwork for Riders

Much of what we just talked about involves the mental processes that restrict our riding. Now we'll take a look at the physical aspects.

As we discussed earlier, compression is one of the main inhibitors of connected riding. Any compression in the rider's spine inhibits the ability of the horse to move freely. If the rider's pelvis is out of balance, compression in the lower spine results. This compressed feeling is then passed along to the horse, making it difficult for him to move freely. Unfortunately, it only takes a minor tilt of the pelvis to restrict movement. Most people don't even know it's happening. So, awareness is key to change.

One of the best ways I've found to help people gain awareness of the concept of compression versus balance is to take them through a series of demonstrations and exercises. Through them, you'll learn what it feels like to be both in balance and out of balance and how to regain that balance once it's lost. The exercises will also teach you expansion (relaxation through proactive movement) and help you improve your body use, and, ultimately, your riding.

Be aware that there are some side effects to this process. You may feel that you aren't doing them right because they're so easy. This is especially daunting for people who are used to working hard to achieve success. You may also feel different in your body. It's not unusual to experience the sensation of being tilted unnaturally forward. This is just your body moving into alignment. So relax and enjoy it. If you don't notice anything right away, don't be discouraged. Your alignment may be off only slightly. Most of us are not used to feeling subtle differences, but your horse will. So be sure to work through all the exercises.

I suggest you find a partner to go through the exercises with you. Your partner can confirm that you're doing the exercises correctly—no matter how easy they are. This is important because what most people percieve as balance is actually counter-balance when they aren't in neutral pelvis position. Your partner can help you find the right position by observing how you hold your body. She'll also be able to assure you that you don't look as though you're ready to fall over when you're in balance! She'll be able to do the exercises after you so you can see and feel what's going on from a different perspective as well. And she'll be there to share your excitement as you begin to integrate connection into your life.

If you don't have a partner, don't worry. You can do most of the exercises by yourself. Whether you work with a partner or not, it's helpful to have a large mirror on hand so you can see what the different positions look like.

Breathing

This first exercise (**Figure 3-1**) will help you understand the importance of breathing when it comes to balance and connection. It's fun and easy. All you need is a kitchen chair and an open mind.

You'll begin by sitting on the edge of the chair. I ask you to do this because this position overrides your habit of "equitating" or "pocket sitting," and allows you to find a new awareness. Remember, we're learning to override our postural habits and replace them with more useful ones that take less effort and create more ease.

Step 1: Take a deep breath. Observe which part of your body expands. Is it your chest? Is it your abdomen? Notice where the breath is coming into your body and how your body feels. Most of us will find that the expansion in this position occurs in the chest because we're used to breathing by lifting the chest. You or your partner should now feel your lower back. Is it hollow, rounded or flat? If it's relaxed, it should be flat.

FIGURE 3-1

Step 2: Next, place your feet shoulder-width apart, lean forward and rest your arms on the top of your thighs. Have your partner place one hand on your lower back and the other on your chest. Breathe deeply. Where does your body expand now? Where do you feel your breath? How does your back feel?

In this position, your lower back and stomach should feel like a balloon is being inflated, and your chest shouldn't lift as you take a breath in. Feel the muscles in your lower back. They should be relaxed.

Through this exercise, we now know that when we

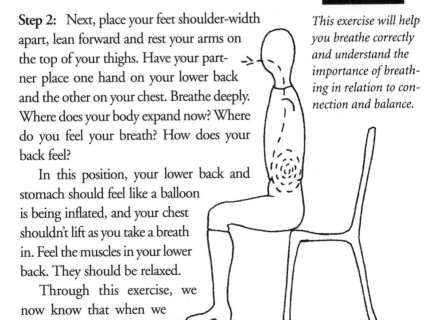

This exercise will help you breathe correctly and understand the importance of breathing in relation to connection and balance.

breathe correctly, the breath enters the abdomen first. A feeling of expansion occurs in the lower back, and continues through the ribs and up into the armpits, allowing the lungs to work efficiently. It also creates a relaxed feeling in the back. Go back and forth between Step 1 and Step 2 several times until you're sure you can identify the difference. Now we'll see if we can capture that same feeling sitting upright.

Step 3: Sit upright on the edge of the chair, and practice breathing deeply into the abdomen and lower back. Have your partner watch what happens. If you're breathing correctly, you'll feel the balloon inflating in your abdomen. It will also create a slightly buoyant feeling. Inhaling will move you back slightly, while exhaling effects a light forward float. This is the neutral position in which your body is in alignment (think of yourself as being "noon" on a clock) and your "hinges" are free for movement.

Can your partner see this movement? Can you feel it? If you're still lifting your chest, blow out as though you were blowing out a candle and try again. Notice that blowing out drops the chest and fills the lower back. Repeat the process until you can do four breaths correctly, but go slowly. Breathing too quickly might make you light-headed. Practice this breathing exercise every day for two weeks. Try to work up to 10 breaths. You'll find that it not only helps you automatically go to the neutral position when you sit, but it's a great way to dissolve stress. If you have a partner, switch places and begin again.

Position

Your body will only bob in the neutral position. It is an imperceptible movement which you can exagerate for someone to see. The horse feels it in an instant. In neutral pelvis your upperbody lightens and your lower half settles and you then sit "deep" without trying. Now that you've discovered the bobbing motion that correct breathing creates, you can put that motion to use in finding your balance (**Figure 3-2**). Remember, when the pelvis is unrestricted, freedom of movement results.

Step 1: Sit on the edge of the chair, breathe into your abdomen, and bob back and forth just a tiny bit. You should be exerting very little effort. You may want to close your eyes so you can concentrate on the feeling. Your partner should confirm that you're moving only slightly as in **Figure 3-2**. Do this for a few seconds and note the feeling. You should feel light and buoyant. It's the motion your body does when you are breathing correctly.

Step 2: Next, sit up very straight. Take a breath. Again, try to keep the motion very small and light. What happens? If you have identified yourself as an Arched Equitator you should pay particular attention to the feeling of this position. Do you still feel light and buoyant? What's going on with your lower back? Does it take more effort to breathe and move? Ask your partner to tell you what she observes, and you should tell her how it feels.

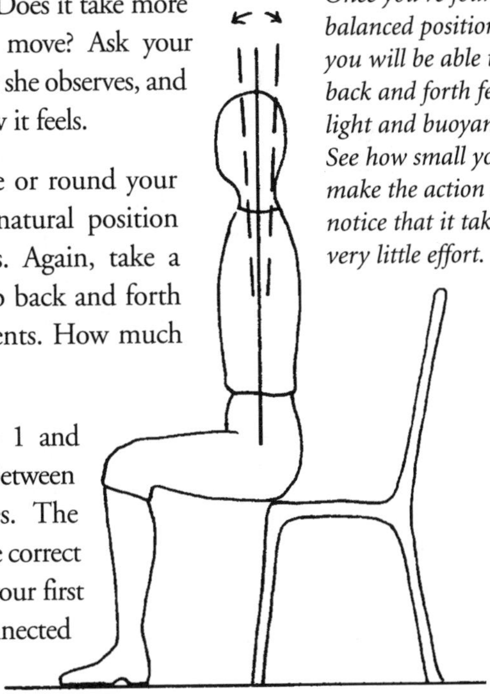

Step 3: Now collapse or round your shoulders. This is a natural position for the Pocket Sitters. Again, take a breath, and try to bob back and forth in very small movements. How much effort does it take?

Step 4: Repeat Step 1 and note the difference between the different postures. The effortless position is the correct one, and finding it is your first step in becoming a connected rider. Recapture this

FIGURE 3-2

Once you've found the balanced position, you will be able to bob back and forth feeling light and buoyant. See how small you make the action and notice that it takes very little effort.

connected position and bob lightly several times a day until it becomes natural for you to sit in this neutral pelvis position. Each time you go out to ride, take a few minutes to sit and "bob" when you get in the saddle. Make sure you adjust your pelvis forward or backward as needed. Bobbing only works when your pelvis is in neutral.

Switch places with your partner and begin again.

Range of Motion

This series of exercises should be done with a partner if possible (**Figure3-3**). If a partner isn't available, you can still give it a try.

Step 1: Stand next to a chair for balancing support, and align your body as though a plumb line were running from your shoulder down through your hip and ankle. Have your partner or your mirror confirm that you're in alignment. Once you're aligned, take a deep breath to relocate the buoyancy and lightness in your upper body. When you're ready, have your partner pick up your leg as though she were picking up a horse's hoof. Make sure you're using your diaphragm as you breathe. It will keep your back relaxed.

Step 2: Next, have your partner move your leg back and forth. What do you feel? If you're properly aligned and balanced, your leg should feel light and easy to move. Experiment with your position until this can be achieved. If

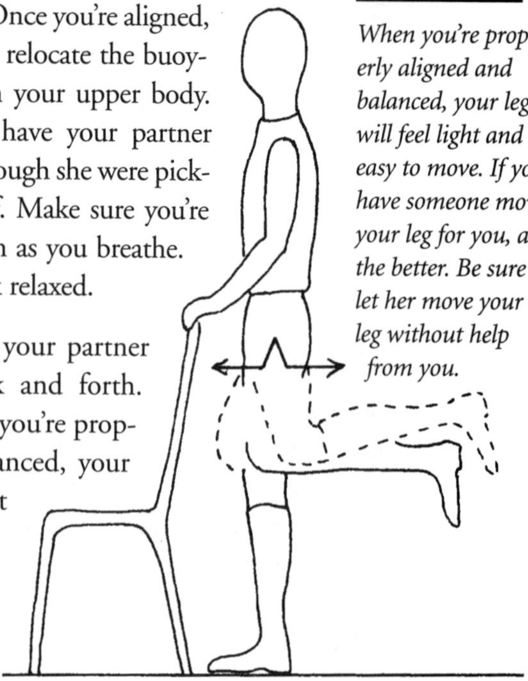

FIGURE 3-3

When you're properly aligned and balanced, your leg will feel light and be easy to move. If you have someone move your leg for you, all the better. Be sure to let her move your leg without help from you.

you're doing these exercises without a partner, simply use the chair for balancing and swing your leg just as a partner would. Note the feeling.

Step 3: While your partner still holds up your leg, change your position to an Arched Equitator by pulling your chest up and arching the small of your back. Now have your partner try to move your leg again. What do you feel? Is your leg heavy and hard to move? Rebalance yourself and see the difference between a balanced movement and the arched posture.

Step 4: Adjust your position again. This time slouch like a Pocket Sitter by pulling your shoulders in and jutting your head forward. As your partner tries to move your leg again, it should feel even heavier and harder to move than before. If you're a Gumby®, your legs will feel looser than the other two positions, but still not as connected as it should be in neutral. Now, rebalance until your leg moves freely once again.

Have your partner repeat all the previous steps so you can feel for yourself the resistance that comes from an unbalanced position.

As you can see from these exercises, a neutral pelvis position gives you the most freedom of movement. This freedom allows you to move with your horse, better communicate with him and guide him with your body. To help reinforce these concepts, study the way people move as you go through your day. Notice how they walk. Do they swing their arms? Do they waddle? How do they carry their heads? Does their movement seem flowing or disconnected?

Also watch the way people stand. Do they stand with their chests high? Do they slump? Are their hips thrust forward? Do they stand with their weight on one leg? Are their knees locked? Do they appear to be tense? Check the plumb line of ear, shoulder, hip and ankle. Develop your eye. It will help you be more aware of how you move and stand and how you sit in the saddle. Becoming aware of your body and how it functions naturally is one of the most important aspects of riding.

Stability

The next set of exercises relates to stability. Everyone wants to feel secure in the saddle. After all, safety is the first rule of riding. But most riders don't realize that a neutral pelvis position also creates stability. This simple exercise (**Figure 3-4**) dramatically illustrates how much more stable our bodies are when in the neutral-pelvis position. This demonstration can be done only with a partner.

Step 1: Begin by standing in the neutral position. Now have your partner apply pressure to your lower back (just below the belt line) using the flat of her hand. Don't resist her push. Notice how much pressure can be applied without having a drastic effect on your balance. While your partner is pushing, add a tiny wiggle or walking-in-place motion with your legs. It should become even more difficult for your partner to push you.

FIGURE 3-4

Standing in neutral position, have your partner press on your lower back just below the belt line. Add a tiny wiggle or walking motion in your legs.

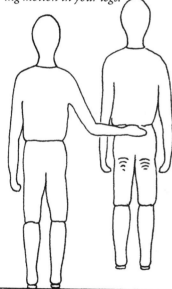

Step 2: Now have your partner instruct you to "Stand up straight." Have your partner then press on your lower back. Don't resist her push. What happens? Don't be surprised if you fall forward, out of balance.

Step 3: Return to the neutral position. Now round your back slightly. Have your partner press on your lower back again. Don't resist. Notice you can still be pushed over—even with just a slight change out of the neutral position. Have your partner repeat the exercise so you can feel how much pressure it takes for movement in the various positions.

Once you and your partner have been through the original exercise, try Steps 2 and 3 again, only this time resist your partner's push. The force of your partner's pressure is like the energy of the horse coming through your body when you're in neutral-pelvis position. Notice how much effort it takes to hold on to a position when you're out of balance versus when you are in neutral-pelvis. It's really a lot of hard work. This is what you're doing to yourself when you ride. Let it go. Try Step 1 again. Notice that it doesn't take effort to stay there as your partner is pressing. This is the lighter, easier way! This is the position of the pelvis that will allow the motion of the horse to go through your body and then back to the horse. This is neutral-pelvis. This will be your position of self-carriage, giving you ease and lightness and freedom during motion.

Communicating With Your Horse

After going through the previous exercises several times, you should be able to identify how a neutral pelvis position feels and be able to find it in yourself when sitting or standing. Now it's time to take that balance and see how it helps us communicate with our horses.

In this first exercise, you'll need a large beach ball or exercise ball. Make sure it's not so big that you can't straddle it and walk with it between your legs (**Figure 3-5**).

Step 1: Place the ball between your legs as if it were your horse's barrel. Your legs should resemble the bend in frog legs. Try walking forward without dropping the ball. Notice that if you squeeze the ball it will "pop" out from between your legs and leave you behind or pop backward, causing you to over react.

Step 2: Now, put yourself in the neutral position and try wiggling your legs in an alternate rhythm as though you were marching in place. Notice that it is easier to move with the ball between your legs when you're released in your spine

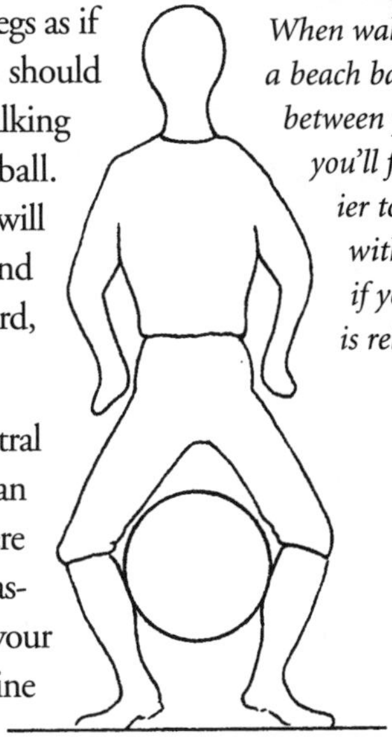

FIGURE 3-5

When walking with a beach ball between your legs, you'll find it easier to move with the ball if your back is released.

and not equitating, slumping or moving excessively like a Gumby®. If you're doing it correctly, it will feel like you're a squatting frog on the ball. In this position you'll be able to move forward with the ball without losing it.

Step 3: Walk around like this for several minutes. Pay close attention to how it feels to use first one leg and then the other. It may be tiring at first, but with practice you should be able to do this easily. Practice every day until it becomes second nature to use your legs in an alternating fashion.

While you're practicing this technique, think about your horse. Most of us are taught to clamp both legs together to squeeze a horse forward. You may have noticed that when you do this, he "pops" right out from under you or he'll resist with a sudden stop, and sometimes you'll fall forward. In either case you will have lost the rhythm. But by relaxing your spine, it allows your legs to move independently of one another, freeing them to follow the motion of the horse's barrel and establishing a connection. This next exercise will demonstrate what we mean (**Figure 3-6**).

Step 1: Stand with knees slightly bent and feet in the position they would be in if you were in the saddle. Make sure you're not hollowing or slumping. Now have your partner kneel or squat in front of you. Next, have your partner cross her hands, placing them on the insides of your calves where the leg would contact the horse. Throughout the exercise, remember that your partner's hands are like the horse's belly.

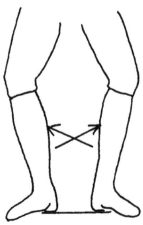

FIGURE 3-6

With your partner's hands playing the part of the horse's belly, walk in place keeping your heels on the ground. If you are released in you spine, your partner will feel a springy motion in her hands that is definitely left-right in nature.

Step 2: Walk in place with your heels on the ground. This stationary walking movement where the soles of your feet remain on the ground simulates your legs around the horse with your feet in the stirrups. If your partner applies a slight amount of pressure on the calves, she will feel a definite left-right motion in her hands. The movement should feel springy and resilient if your back is released and your pelvis is in a balanced position. When your partner applies pressure, you can move her hand with your legs. Also notice how your shock-absorbing "hinges" (soles, ankles, knees and hips) feel. They should all be open and moving and your soles should feel like they are really connected to the ground as pressure is applied.

Step 3: Now change your position to arched, then slouched. Your partner should observe that the motion becomes jarring and she'll lose the left-right motion. You'll also lose your ability to move her hands. If your partner applies pressure with her hands, it will move your leg instead. Also notice that your hinges are no longer free and the soles of your feet feel unstable. You've just lost communication and control, freedom of motion and independent use of the two sides of your body.

Step 4: Change positions with your partner. This time you'll be the horse. Can you feel the difference when your partner moves from a balanced position to an out-of-balance position? If not, check your partner's posture to make sure she starts out in neutral. Adjust her position and try again.

By now you should begin to see how freedom in your body can open up or close down communication with your horse. In this next exercise, you'll be able to actually feel what your horse feels when you ride in or out of connection. For this demonstration you'll need a partner, a small exercise trampoline and something to simulate reins, such as a rope or scarf. If a trampoline is not available, try a springy couch cushion (**Figure 3-7**).

Step 1: Stand in the center of the trampoline with feet flat, shoulder-width apart. Your partner, or "horse," should stand in front, facing forward, holding the pretend reins about waist high. Take the reins in your hands just as though you were in the saddle and find neutral position. (If you have trouble finding neutral, release and soften the back by taking an inhaling breath up the spine, filling the lower back first and breathing out as if you were blowing out a candle. This will allow the spine to soften, which will release the hips. Use this technique any time you need to rebalance, either in or out of the saddle. It will bring your body back to plumb.)

Step 2: Walk in place with your soles remaining on the trampoline, keeping your feet flat. Your step should be springy and light. If it's flat and heavy, you're probably out of balance. Once you're in balance again, what do you notice in the reins? Can you feel a slight left/right motion? Ask your "horse" to close her eyes and tell you what she feels.

FIGURE 3-7

In this exercise remember to keep your heels on the surface of the trampoline. Your knees can bend without lifting your heels.

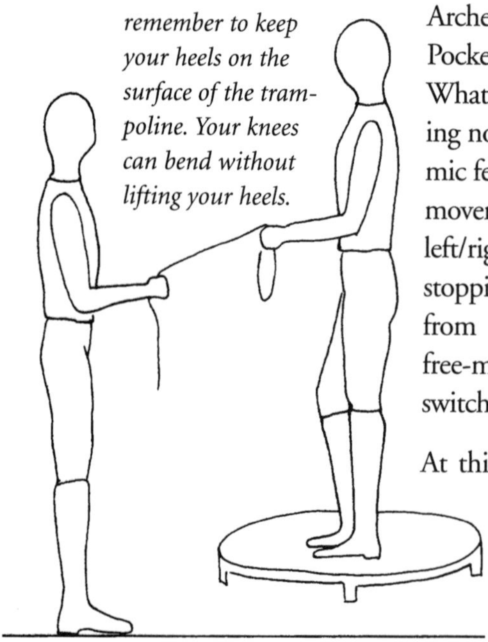

Step 3: While maintaining your walking rhythm, stiffen your back as if you're an Arched Equitator or slump as if you're a Pocket Sitter. Gumbies should do both. What happens? What is your partner feeling now? Do you still get a smooth rhythmic feeling through "the reins" or are your movements jarring to the horse? Is the left/right motion still there? Now without stopping, try to rebalance. Practice going from free-moving to stiff to slumped to free-moving again several times. Then switch places with your partner.

At this point in my clinics, students are usually very animated. Connection works! It's exciting to gain some understanding of how little it takes to communicate with

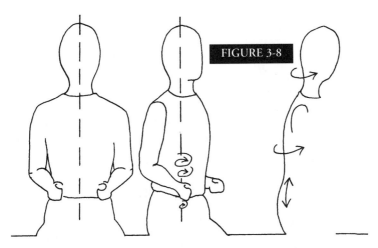

FIGURE 3-8

Feel the difference between rotating your upper body on an even turn around a central axis, and twisting which is common and undesirable. Rotation is always accompanied by a release in the lower back. Your spring will feel like a corkscrew swirling around the central axis. Notice that your hands, if held in riding position, follow the rotation of the upper body and that the shoulders don't lead the movement.

your horse. Remember, if a horse can feel a fly on his back, it's a pretty good bet he gets the message without our squeezing and pulling on him. The next demonstration shows just how little we have to do to tell a horse where we want him to go (**Figure 3-8**).

Step 1: Resume your positions as rider and horse. Find neutral. Begin "riding" (walking in place).

Step 2: Once you've established your rhythm and your horse can feel your left/right motion through the reins, ask your partner to close her eyes. Continue in rhythm for a few seconds, and then smoothly rotate your upper body to the left. Pretend there's a searchlight in the center of your chest, and keep your eyes in line with your searchlight. Make sure your lower body stays released. Think forward as though you want to buoy back to the plumb line. (Moving, when you are accustomed to being stiff or slouched, takes your body behind the plumb line.) Maintain rhythm.

Step 3: Now rotate back to center. Stay there for a few seconds and then smoothly rotate your upper body to your right. Repeat the rotation back to the center, then left and back to center.

If you've been in neutral pelvis position, your partner has probably been involuntarily turning in the direction of your upper body. And all you did was rotate in the direction you wanted to go! Now it's your turn to be the horse. Switch places and begin again.

Meet and Melt

The final concept we need to cover in this chapter is "meet and melt". This teaches you how to connect with the horse to bring him back to you when he's doing something unwanted, like hanging or dropping the bit or going above it. It also allows you to ride with a soft rein and "check in" with your horse to let him know you're still there.

The concept behind meet and melt is simple (**Figure 3-9**). When you "meet" you match the pressure that the horse is exerting on the reins. You "melt" by very slowly softening the muscles in your back, ribcage and arms that you just used to "meet".

FIGURE 3-9

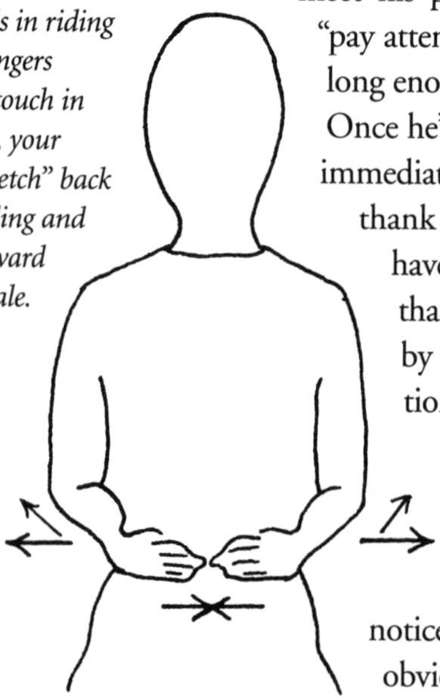

With hands in riding position, fingers opened to touch in the middle, your elbows "stretch" back upon inhaling and "melt" forward as you exhale.

This gives your horse two messages. First of all, when you meet his pressure, you're saying "no" or "pay attention." You want to do this just long enough to get your message across. Once he's started to relax or release, you immediately melt and say "that's right, thank you." Horses would rather have the release, so when they learn that they can be in a released state by rebalancing and paying attention, they listen to you more readily. The other wonderful aspect of "meet and melt" is that it doesn't take any strength to execute, is barely noticeable to an observer but very obvious to the receiver.

Try this: Sit on the edge of a chair and find your neutral pelvis position for the breathing exercise. Now place your arms and hands in a riding position with fingers open and touching. Breathe in and out from the abdomen. What's happening with your arms? That's right. When you inhale your elbows "stretch" back as though they were elastic, and as you exhale they "melt" forward—"meet and melt".

As you become more comfortable with this concept, you can control how slowly you soften and melt, giving your horse time to rebalance without being rigid or held up by a tight rein. Ideally the melt takes three times the amount of time it takes you to meet—or about six seconds. When very refined, "meet" becomes an inhalation felt through the reins and "melt" an exhalation, giving the horse a subtle rhythm with which to move. When the horse is balanced and released through the spine, the "meet and melt" becomes a part of the reciprocal dance of rhythm and rebalancing that is a subconscious sharing of true partnership.

To demonstrate "meet and melt", let's do one final exercise. This will be easiest to do sitting on the edge of a chair, feet set shoulder-width apart or straddling a bench. Your partner should be in front of you at a lower level, facing forward, pretend reins in place.

Step 1: To begin, establish a light contact in a balanced position. March your legs in a walking motion with your soles on the ground.

Step 2: Have your partner apply pressure to or slacken the reins, just as a horse might do.

Step 3: Meet the contact equally. In other words, if the horse is pulling his head forward, try to meet that same pressure by stretching your elbows back. As you're stretching back through your elbows, think forward as if you were bobbing slightly as described on page 42, to override any tendency to stiffen. Then slowly soften the muscles under the arms and rib cage to melt.

Repeat this two or three times to make sure you understand the concept.

Step 4: Now pull on the reins as though you were pulling on a horse's mouth. Notice that this starts from the hand and requires a tight wrist and back. You're no longer connected to the horse in a light, natural way. Now you're in a tug of war with him and chances are, if he wants you to lose, you will.

Step 5: Rebalance and try to imagine your arms and reins forming a funnel for your horse to move into and through. If your spine is released as you ride, your elbows are being moved by the walking motion. This is automatic and will move your elbows imperceptibly left and right with the horse's movement.

You also need to pay attention to your wrists. Try to release or lighten your wrists just by thinking them lighter. Relax and think (don't actually do) left, right, left, right. Meet. Melt. Don't be surprised if you find yourself "riding" from the edge of the chair!

Practice this as often as you can. You won't always need a partner. Try rigging up a set of pretend reins somewhere in your house. I find a scarf tied to a dresser drawer pull works well. If you pull too hard, the draw pops open, so that helps to keep your touch light.

That takes us through our basic rider groundwork exercises. There is a lot to absorb, so go through the exercises and demonstrations more than once to be sure you fully understand them and feel comfortable with your breathing, neutral pelvis position and communication. A note of caution: I don't recommend going back to the incorrect postures once you've begun the process of finding lightness and ease. At a deeper level you're retraining your nervous system and you want to put in good information. So once you've felt the difference between the positions, stay with the neutral position for your exercises. That way the body will remember to remember. And you'll begin to understand that less effort means more achievement.

Now let's put what we've learned to use in the saddle.

Chapter 4

Saddle Up

"The only constant is change.
The only freedom is movement"
Peggy Cummings

Finally it's time to get on your horse. Well, almost. Before we actually saddle up, I'd like to talk about the saddle itself. You've seen advertising that proclaims, "Your saddle—it's the only thing that should come between you and your horse." That's right. That's why having a saddle that fits is so important.

As I work with people across the country, I find that at least a portion of their riding problems stem from something other than their riding techniques. Sometimes it's poor equine dental care (imagine a bit in your mouth if you have a toothache!). Sometimes it's poor nutrition. Sometimes it's improper shoeing. Any one of these things affects how a horse can and will move and perform. But more often than not, people are using saddles that just don't fit.

This problem is so prevalent that in a clinic with 12 new people, nine or 10 will have a poorly fitting saddle. That's 80 percent! What's really sad is that often these people have just purchased their saddles and had them "custom" fitted to their horses. To make sure you aren't going to face challenges connecting with your horse because of your

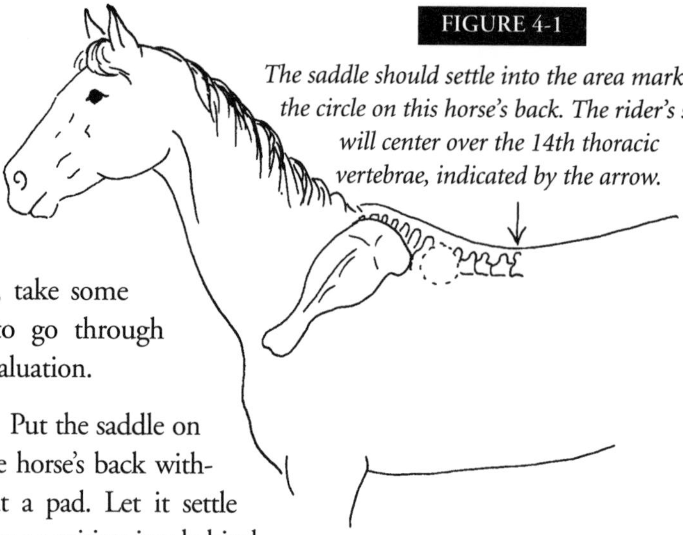

FIGURE 4-1

The saddle should settle into the area marked by the circle on this horse's back. The rider's seat will center over the 14th thoracic vertebrae, indicated by the arrow.

saddle, take some time to go through this evaluation.

1. Put the saddle on the horse's back without a pad. Let it settle into a position just behind the shoulder blade. This will allow the rider's seat to be over the 14th thoracic vertebrae (**Figure 4-1**).

2. From the front of your horse, look down the gullet of the saddle. The top of the panel should lie along the top of the back on either side of the spine. If the panel is higher than the spine at any point, the saddle is too narrow or the tree doesn't fit. If the panel lies one quarter of an inch lower than either side of the spine, the saddle is too wide (**Figure 4-2**).

3. Looking down the gullet, you should be able to see all the way from the front to the back of the saddle. The panels of the saddle should be lying on either side of the spine. If there is a gap in the middle the saddle is bridging (**Figure 4-3**).

4. Next, check the withers area. Place three to four fingers together and slide them in between the withers and the pommel to measure clearance. When the girth is tight and you're sitting in the saddle, you should always be able to slide in three fingers.

5. Now check the shoulder area. The saddle should not interfere with the shoulder. The point of the tree should be positioned

behind the rear of the scapula (shoulder). With a flat hand under the pommel, move down along the shoulder area. Is the saddle tight against the shoulder, or is there clearance for the shoulder to move naturally? If it's tight, try moving the saddle back first. If you still have trouble clearing your hand under the front flap, your saddle is interfering with the shoulder's range of motion (**Figure 4-4**).

6. A saddle shouldn't press into the loin area. Some western and endurance saddles are too long for some horses' backs. And some poorly made English saddles have an edge instead of a rounded panel system that digs into the horse's back. Make sure there are at least four inches—or a flat-hand distance—between the back of the western saddle and the point of the hip. Be sure nothing is digging into your horse's back.

7. From the rear, check that there is no contact with the spinal area, just as you did for the front in Step 2. The tree should stabilize on either side of the spine but never contact the spine. Some saddles, especially jumping saddles, are narrower through the gullet in the middle and the panels press on the spine.

8. Finally, check for stability. The saddle shouldn't teeter or rock from front to back or side to side. It should be stable and level.

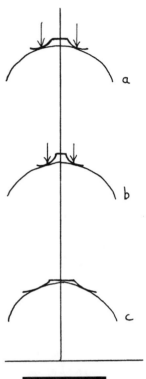

FIGURE 4-2

The saddle panels should lie evenly along the top of the back on either side of the spine (a). Two narrow a saddle sets the panels higher than the spine (b) which will cause pinching pressure. Too wide (c) sets the panels low and eliminates clearance for the back.

If your saddle passes all these tests, that's great! But if it doesn't, you need help. Dense, foam-rubber shims and pads can be used under

FIGURE 4-3

An even distribution of weight is desirable along the horse's back (a).

a

Bridging results from panels that don't touch in the middle between front and back (b). This problem often goes unnoticed.

b

your saddle to correct saddle fit, but you have to know what you're doing. It is a temporary solution. Be sure to keep checking your horse's back. A thicker pair of wool socks in a pair of shoes that fit or are too small won't give you more comfort. And if you put a wedge in your shoe to alleviate some discomfort and that wedge creates an uncomfortable seam, you haven't gained anything. So be careful what you do.

If you use a shim to fill a gap, make sure it's not creating another problem. The same goes for corrective pads used to change the shape and size of the horse's back. These can help avoid some problems, but they have to be used properly. Some padding can absorb shock, which also may help. But remember, nonfunctional or straight padding simply adds another layer of poor fit—just like

Even when the girth or cinch is tightened and the rider's weight is in the saddle, you should be able to slide three fingers in under the pommel (a). Your flat hand should slide easily in under the saddle (b) and down under the flap.

the thick socks. There should never be any added pressure on the horse's spine, so watch for pads that are too heavy or aren't fitted to allow room through the gullet.

If you're having trouble getting a saddle to fit, you may want to talk to a real saddle-fitting expert (not just someone who sells saddles). In most cases, the fit can be corrected. The exception is a saddle that's too small. Nothing but a new saddle can help that. If you're faced with a saddle that just doesn't fit and can't be corrected, look for one that does fit. The expense of an unsound or unsafe horse is far greater than that of a properly fitting saddle.

Getting Ready to Ride

Now that you know your equipment is good for the horse, you can prepare to ride. Getting ready to ride doesn't mean just tacking up and heading to the arena. If you're looking for the best ride, you should first stretch, practice a few balancing exercises and prepare yourself mentally to connect with your horse. This doesn't have to take long—just a few minutes. Mary Midkiff's book *Fitness, Performance and the Female Equestrian* (Howell Book House, New York, 1996) takes riders through a series of exercises to help prepare their bodies for riding. Horses should also stretch and loosen. TTEAM™ work and *Connected Ground Exercises*™ are a big help in getting your horse ready to ride. They're all worth looking into.

For now though, let's just make sure that both your upper and lower body are stretched out before mounting and that your horse has had an opportunity to work out his kinks. Then take a few deep breaths using your diaphragm, and visualize yourself moving in harmony with your horse. While preparing your horse to ride, check him over to make sure nothing is hurting him, bothering him, or putting him in a bad mood. Even horses have a bad day now and then. This prep time is a good way to make sure everything is in order.

Once your preparation is completed, it's time to climb on board. To mount, use a mounting block, bale of straw or some other safe, stable device that allows you to lift into the saddle without twisting the saddle out of shape (especially English saddles), putting too much pressure on the horse's back or too much strain on your own body. (It's not "sissy" to use a mounting block—it's smart.) If possible, have a partner with you on your first day. We'll begin by going through exercises similar to the ones you did in the last chapter, only this time astride the horse.

Releasing Your Back

As we discussed in previous chapters, it's impossible to achieve a connected ride with a stiff back. And while you've done your homework, and know what a released back feels like off the horse, sometimes getting in the saddle triggers old habits of riding. This first exercise will help you to feel the balanced, released sensation while you are mounted.

> **Step 1:** While mounted, have your partner place her hand on your back and slowly stroke from the shoulder blades down to the small of your back on either side of the spine. Do this a few times to imprint the feel of your spine and back muscles. Now, focus on the small of your back. Sense how it feels when you're in your familiar riding position. Is there tension? Does it feel

tight or rigid? Is there a deep curve? Is your back rounded? Remember, your lower back can't release unless your back muscles are free of tension.

Step 2: Take a deep breath into your abdomen. Exhale and feel your body settle. An expanded, full feeling should take place. Does your back feel different?

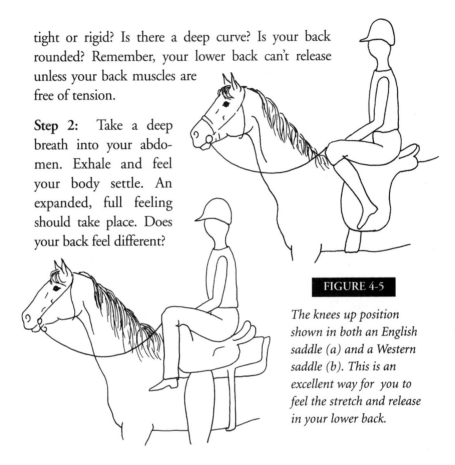

FIGURE 4-5

The knees up position shown in both an English saddle (a) and a Western saddle (b). This is an excellent way for you to feel the stretch and release in your lower back.

Don't be discouraged if you're having trouble getting your back to release. Remember, you're overcoming some very ingrained habits. This next exercise might help you get over this first hurdle (**Figure 4-5**).

Step 1: Drop your stirrups and place your knees together at the pommel. Think about your seat bones in the saddle. Feel them; are they even?

Step 2: Remaining in the knees-up position (**Figure 4-5**), ask your partner to place her hand in the small of your back. It should feel smooth, full and soft. The tension should be gone. *Note:* If you're used to hollowing your back, you'll

FIGURE 4-6

This is the "frog on the ball" idea. In order to surround the horse, you need to feel wide through the hips. When you "cuddle" or "surround" the belly, your knees will lift up slightly and your calves will come in under the barrel.

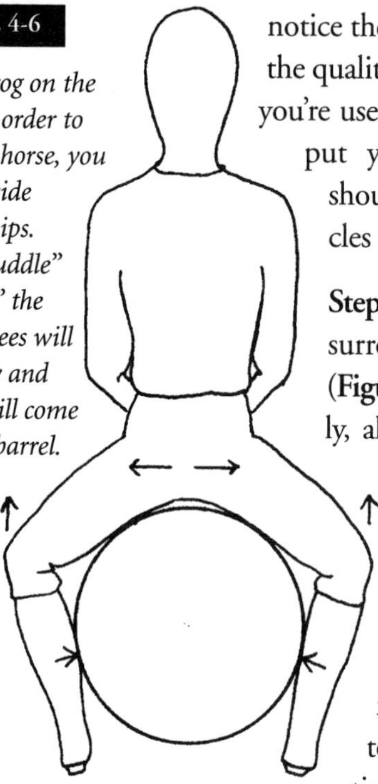

notice the hollow feeling has changed and the quality of the muscles feels different. If you're used to rounding your back, as you put your upper body upright you should feel a difference in those muscles as well.

Step 3. Now slowly drop your legs to surround the barrel of the horse (**Figure 4-6**). Raise your knees slightly, allowing your calves to touch the horse's belly. Your back should feel more relaxed.

Lower Body Position

Next, we'll make sure your seat is in the best place to allow movement and your legs are free to act independently. This position will allow you to establish communication with your horse. Before you begin, have your partner press on your lower back (below the waist) as she did in Chapter 3. If your upper body moves slightly, you're not in the neutral position. If this happens, scoot your seat bones forward. You may only need to scoot forward (or backward, depending on your habitual posture) an eighth of an inch.

Now have your partner press on your back again. When you're in the neutral pelvic position, a lot of pressure can be added to your lower back without your upper body moving. You'll feel secure, comfortable and solid unless your saddle isn't balanced or user friendly. Once you've found your neutral position you can begin the exercise.

Step 1: With your foot out of the stirrup, have your partner gently take your ankle in one hand and support your bent knee with the other (**Figure 4-7**) and bring your leg slightly back and under you. If your pelvis is in the neutral position,

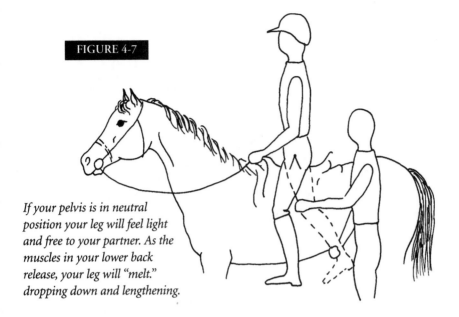

FIGURE 4-7

If your pelvis is in neutral position your leg will feel light and free to your partner. As the muscles in your lower back release, your leg will "melt." dropping down and lengthening.

your leg will move easily, your buttocks won't feel restricted and your upper body will be independently stable. It should be easy to find your "bob."

Step 2: Take a deep breath and let it out. Concentrate on allowing your neck and back to release (soften).

Step 3: As your partner feels the release that the breathing created, she'll notice that your leg starts to sink. She should follow your leg as it slowly drops. When this happens, the leg will feel like it's "melting." This feeling is a result of the muscles in your pelvis and lower back releasing. Your partner should feel your leg lengthen and drop into balance. If it doesn't, try a very small, quick scoot forward or backward in the saddle, and take a deep breath using your diaphragm. Continue adjusting and breathing until your partner can easily and slowly move your leg back and forth as demonstrated in the groundwork range-of-motion exercises.

Step 4: Once you're properly balanced in the neutral position, have your partner place a hand under your foot just behind the

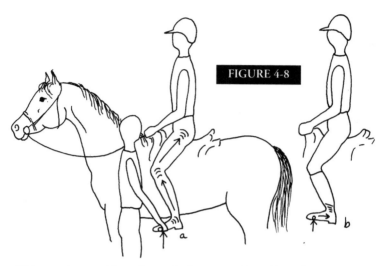

FIGURE 4-8

This exercise provides a dramatic demonstration of how free the "hinges" in your leg and hip can be when the pelvis is unrestricted. With your partner's hand behind the ball of the foot, bounce the foot. The bounce will travel all the way into your hip (a). From the ball of the foot, (b) is the pelvis is restricted when the foot is bounced the bounce travels back to the heel and is lost in a jarring action in the ankles.

ball of the foot. Relax and allow her to bounce your leg up and down. If she can do this easily, your "hinges" are working and there is a spring in all the joints. You should be able to feel the movement all the way up into your hip joint (**Figure 4-8**).

Now that your seat and legs are balanced, let's look at the feet. Often we're told to push down our heels in riding. While this might add some security, it really only serves to lock the ankle hinge, which in turn locks the hip and pelvis. True security comes with dynamic, balanced motion and the ability to rebalance in motion. Remember the stability exercise? When you're balanced, it's hard to unseat you. So to maintain yourself in balance, allow your feet to be level in the stirrup.

Step 1: Place your feet in the stirrups. Have your partner position your foot so that it's parallel to the ground. The stirrup should be about just behind the ball joint to maintain flexibility and movement.

Step 2: Have your partner bounce your leg again to test your freedom of movement. Once this is achieved, position and test the other side.

In this position, your foot can act as a shock absorber, allowing your body to receive and move with the horse's motion. You'll be more secure and connected as you settle down into your sole. You'll also keep the line of communication open by not closing off the ankle joint.

Upper Body Position

So far, we've been concentrating on the lower body. Now it's time to take a look above the waist. We'll begin with releasing the neck and shoulders.

Step 1: Bring both hands down to your side and let your arms dangle. Turn your palms up and notice how your arms move while hanging down. Next, turn the palms out, facing forward, and then under, facing back. Notice that the rotation of the hand melts the tense shoulder. There's no clamping in the armpit after this exercise (**Figure 4-9**).

FIGURE 4-9

Rotating your palms with your arms hanging down will release any tension in your shoulder.

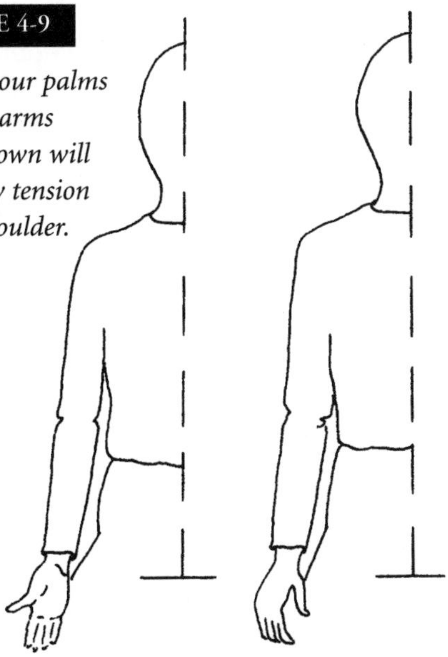

Step 2: Imagine you're inside a fish tank. Touch the walls parallel to your ears (**Figure 4-10**). Push against the wall, hold for a few seconds, relax and repeat. This exercise softens the collar bone and shoulder area.

Step 3: Now, slowly bring your arms back around into the riding position. You'll find they lie flat against your body and your joints remain more flexible.

If your shoulders are very tight, you may have trouble getting them to open. If that's the case, try this:

Step 1: Imagine you have a piece of bubble gum sitting on the top of each shoulder (**Figure 4-11**). Now place your fingers on the gum and pull it slowly up and out with bent elbows and imagine the string of bubble gum following.

Step 2: Slowly bring your arms down the sides of your body and around until your elbows are resting at your sides and your hands are in the correct riding position in relation to the withers.

This exercise puts you in a relaxed position with shoulders centered and square over your hips. At the beginning of the exercise your arms may have felt heavy, but when you breathe and let your arms down slowly, they will automatically lighten and feel more open.

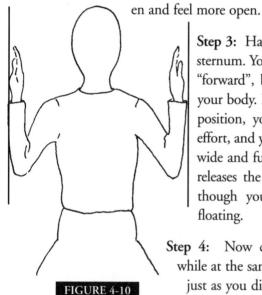

FIGURE 4-10

A good exercise to release tension in your shoulders. If you create tension in your back when doing this one, bring your hands forward a little and try again.

Step 3: Have your partner press on your sternum. You should respond by thinking "forward", breathing and staying soft in your body. If your pelvis is in the neutral position, you'll remain upright without effort, and your back will continue to feel wide and full. When your partner slowly releases the pressure, you should feel as though you're lightening, levitating or floating.

Step 4: Now continue thinking "forward" while at the same time "marching" your legs just as you did with the ball between your legs. You should feel solid, free and very excited. You've just learned how to do two things simultaneously—think forward and march—while overriding the habit of stiffening as movement begins.

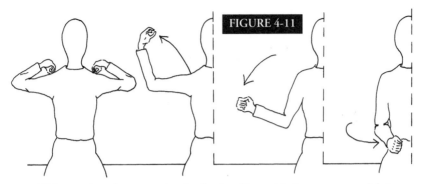

This exercise releases tension in the shoulders and gives you a good feel for how your arms can hang naturally at your side.

Rebalancing

This exercise incorporates the floating or bobbing exercises we learned in Chapter 3. Through it we will not only learn to find neutral but also to regain balance often during our ride. Why? Because the horse is dynamic—that is, moving all the time—so our balanced position will always be challenged by his movement. Remember, in riding the only constant is change through movement.

Rebalancing takes place in exactly the same way that balance was achieved in the first place (**Figure 4-12**).

> **Step 1:** Imagine yourself "floating" forward with your upper body. Take a deep breath into your diaphragm and imagine you're blowing out a candle located right between your horse's ears.

> **Step 2:** Slowly allow your chest to soften, and feel your back fill as you exhale.

> **Step 3:** Check to see if you're feeling that slight bobbing back and forth that you experienced in your groundwork. Notice how this feels.

At any point during your riding you can rebalance just like this. Imagine yourself floating forward or blowing out a candle (think forward). Then check the independent movement of your legs

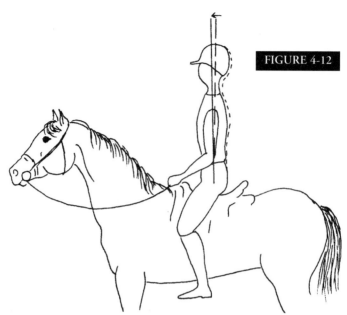

FIGURE 4-12

Finding this unrestricted and balanced position isn't hard. You've felt it during the exercises and can find it in the saddle. When your pelvis is in the neutral position, you can effortlessly buoy forward as described earlier. Think of a motion picture in stop-action and take yourself one frame forward. Be careful not to break your axis at the rib cage. Feel tall and wide in your collar bone and breathe into your abdomen. The feeling is light and the marching action in your legs will come easily. This is the feeling of balance you want to return to every stride.

(march). Think forward and march. Put this in your mind. It really works. Before long you'll be doing it automatically every time you feel yourself out of balance. You will respond to change by softening your body and moving without rigidity.

All of the work so far has been designed to help you find and re-find a connected position in the saddle. It might seem like a lot to go through, but if you're not in alignment with ease, you can't communicate with your horse. This connected position is not familiar to most riders, so we must know what it feels like in order to attain it.

So now that you're gaining awareness and freedom and have stored the feeling in your muscle memory banks (repetition is the best way to build muscle memory and good habits), you're ready to communicate.

Chapter 5

Making the Connection

"Today all I could remember was the way your
body held the ocean of myself and for a
moment there was only one of us in all creation."

Brian Andreas,
Strange Dreams

The frustrating thing about a book on basics is that you have to learn the basics before you can move ahead to the fun work. But you've applied yourself, so now you're ready to be rewarded with one of the most wonderful feelings in the world—harmony in motion.

I'll never forget one student who waited until she was 50 years old to finally get her first horse. It had been a childhood dream that had taken her half a century to fulfill. After two years of working with her Paso Fino, Minnow, she came to a clinic hoping to improve her riding and her relationship with her horse. For four days she listened and worked, intent on taking in every nuance of release and balance. The clinics are intense for everyone because so much is covered, but Linda persevered. Later, I got a letter from her about her clinic experience.

She wrote: "While I was focusing on releasing my back, float-ing forward to go with the movement, keeping my elbows light and "stretchy," holding my hands correctly and quietly "fluffing" with my lower legs, something else happened. For just a few seconds, I experienced being "one" with Minnow in movement. That unity of movement, as I said at the time with tears in my eyes, was very moving. It felt like something I had come into this life to experience and that I had been looking for my whole life, without really knowing it until that moment." Linda is not alone.

Connecting with your horse, and opening up the lines of com-munication that let you lead your partner in the dance of riding is what each of us has been working toward. So let's begin with one of the most important concepts in *Connected Riding®*—something I call "Ta-daa."

Ta-daa

When I first introduce this principle, some people look at me as though I am a little nuts. I can see they want to say, "What a silly word". Maybe so, but there is a method to the madness of ta-daa. In learning new habits, it's helpful to use vocabulary that is non-habitual. For example, if I'm teaching you to use your leg in a dif-ferent way, I'll show you what I mean and let you experience the feeling of the new position. That's good. But if I then use an old command—even though it's asking for the new position—the sub-conscious will go back to the old way of using the leg. So that's why I introduce new words for the concepts of *Connected Riding®*. The words don't really matter. They just have to be something you're not used to. So, on to ta-daa (**Figure 5-1**).

As with everything else in *Connected Riding®*, the principle behind ta-daa is based on biomechanics. Basically it's a subtle and irresistible one/two communication from your muscles to those of the horse. This communication is initiated by a very slight "march-ing" movement of the thighs—something like pedaling backward on a unicycle. Your feet remain in the irons, while your hip, knee,

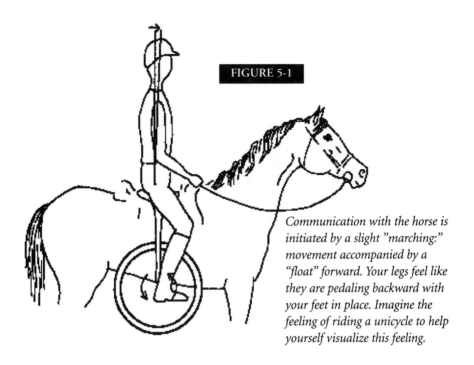

FIGURE 5-1

Communication with the horse is initiated by a slight "marching:" movement accompanied by a "float" forward. Your legs feel like they are pedaling backward with your feet in place. Imagine the feeling of riding a unicycle to help yourself visualize this feeling.

ankle and arch joints do the moving. It's not hard. Remember the exercises you did with the ball between your legs in Chapter 3? Or the exercises you did in Chapter 4 to help you establish independence in your legs? This result is what they were building toward.

Just think of the horse as a ball between your legs. With first one leg and then the other, slightly flex your leg muscles thinking ta-daa or one, two. It should feel almost like a shiver or vibratory muscular movement that begins with the back-pedaling, up-and-down movement of your thighs and runs down through your calves. The horse feels the movement along his barrel and this signals him to move forward smoothly. From the ground it's barely perceptible, but from the back of the horse it's a powerful movement. So powerful, in fact, I've found that even a horse who has been stuck or stiff for a long time finds it irresistible. This vibratory movement—which will need to be fairly strong for a "stuck" horse—overrides or shakes up the "cement" in a horse, just like an earthquake breaks up a building.

It's remarkable. Just think how wonderful it would be to be able to get a horse to move forward just by shivering your legs. No more spurs. No more kicking. No more slaps on the rear. Just ta-daa. It's really that simple.

Creating Motion

In *Connected Riding*®, when you want your horse to move forward, you don't squeeze your legs to produce movement. You encourage movement in the horse by awakening his own natural left/right motion of the hind legs by using ta-daa. The same is true when encouraging your horse to pay attention or pick up the pace. Again, you don't squeeze. You "fast forward" your own movement to encourage him to catch up with you. It's as if you were saying to him, "come on" through your legs.

Now let's try it. Remember to adjust your seat to the neutral position as soon as you get in the saddle.

Step 1: Begin by taking a deep breath into your diaphragm. Be careful not to raise your chest. Then stretch back your elbows lightly to make a connection with your horse.

Step 2: Ta-daa to direct your horse to move forward, and blow out the candle to allow your body to float forward into balance. As you inhale slightly, rotate your body one or two degrees. Then soften the muscles you contracted in Step 1 to stretch your elbows back. This release of muscles is like saying "Thank you" to your horse for paying attention and doing what you asked. It also allows the horse to find his own self-carriage.

Step 3: Let your legs and seat follow the horse's movement.

As your horse moves out smoothly, you are in sync with his motion. Feel him under you? Left, right. Left, right. A true connection. And by using his own motion to encourage movement, the horse can expand and release his spine, which in turn rounds and softens his frame. This builds the power of the push of the hind leg to move forward with energy and ease. It feels good to you. It feels good to the horse. And you're actually teaching and allowing your horse to walk his hind legs up under you. It's like revving up an engine—and it's what *Connected Riding®* is all about. Release (think forward and rotate), Connect (stretch the elbows), Come on (ta-daa) and Thank you (allowing) (**Figure 5-2**).

These four steps compose a cycle for horse and rider that not only starts motion but is the means of rebalancing and forming a partnership through your ride. Release, Rotate, Connect, Ta-daa or Come on, Thank You. The cycle is complete in a matter of seconds, as long as it takes to take a deep breath and blow it out again.

Think about each of the steps in a way that makes sense to you. Rename them if you want. If "breathe," "swivel," "contact," "wiggle" and "allow" work for you, that's just fine. Think the steps in order and make up a mantra to recite and repeat in your mind until asking a horse to move forward this way—one, two, three, four—is as natural as breathing. In time you'll find the feeling before you even think the words.

Connecting the Walk

At first we'll work at the walk so you can concentrate on what you're doing without having to deal with the demands of the trot. I know going back to walk work is like being put back a grade in school for some, but be patient. Accomplished athletes in all sports, including basketball, football, tennis and yes, riding, go back to the basics on a regular basis. Shoring up the foundation is vital to success in any endeavor.

When I watched dressage master Reiner Klimke teach in Pennsylvania in 1990, he kept stressing the importance of the basics, including a good walk. It didn't matter what level rider with whom he was working. He did the same foundation work for training-level riders as he did for Grand Prix riders. We should all take this lesson from the master to heart.

Step 1: Sit on your horse with your body in the neutral position. Keep a hand on the reins, just to have them handy, but try not to use them. Repeat your mantra: Release and Rotate, Connect, Come On, Thank You. Have someone with you who

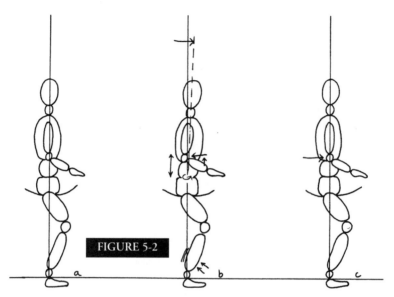

The cycle of connection begins in a balanced position (a). RELEASE, let go in your back, rotate and float forward one frame. CONNECT, by thinking back with your elbows and lightening your forearm. COME ON, by "marching" with your legs, alternating right and left (b). THANK YOU, by releasing the muscles you contracted when you stretched your elbows back (c).

can lead the horse. Walk a short time with your eyes closed so you can really feel the balance and motion.

Think about the steps of rebalancing as you let the horse walk and you follow the movement.

Step 2: With your eyes still closed and your partner leading the horse, revert back to your habitual riding style. Feel what happens when you stiffen up or do something that used to be familiar, like slouch. How does your horse feel? How did he react when you reverted?

Step 3: Now open your eyes and take the reins, doing the sequence on your own. Release and Rotate, Connect, Come On, Thank You. You should feel the horse step under and make an effort to accentuate the push of his hind legs as you ta-daa. Is this different from what you're used to? How does the horse react?

Step 4: Try your old position and see how your horse reacts. Do this only for a moment. We don't want to reinforce old habits. Then go back to the connected walk, and walk around the arena long enough to feel the difference.

As you repeat these exercises, leave out the part where you return to your old riding habits. Initially, the purpose was to help you feel the difference, but we don't want to reinforce bad habits while we're trying to incorporate new ones.

One Degree At A Time

The purpose of this exercise is to give you practice in rotating with a released back and thinking forward while maintaining your marching movement. It also helps the horse release and soften through the withers and pelvis. As you're doing this exercise, remember the trampoline exercises where we introduced the searchlight in your chest.

Step 1: Release, Rotate, Connect, Come On, Thank You to connect you and your horse. This step will send him forward in a relaxed, energetic walk that begins in the hind end.

Step 2: As you move forward, rotate your body slowly (remember the searchlight) in increments like the second hand on a watch, three increments either left or right—moving first to one side, back to middle and then to the other side. If you're completely relaxed and your hinges are loose, your body will move just as it did in the rider groundwork exercises. Notice that the rotation of the torso changes the position of your leg and elbow at each increment of rotation. This is very subtle. Your upper thighs should move slightly as you rotate. But make sure you're allowing them to move, and not making them move. Remember, it's the movement of the horse that should enable your legs to continue the marching motion that began with ta-daa.

Step 3: Continue to walk along on a loose rein, rotating the upper body one, two, three increments to the left. Then one, two, three back to the center. Repeat to the right and then back to the center. Remember to keep your eyes looking in the direction of your chest—just as if you were following the searchlight.

How did your horse react? As you passed the middle and rotated to the inside, your horse should have released his head and neck and lengthened his topline (raising the base). (Most horses respond to the connection automatically.) Then on a long rein, try circle left, circle right, and maneuvers through an obstacle course. You can still continue doing one degree at a time through the turns. If you go through this routine at the beginning of each ride, you'll both start your day off on the right path—connected and ready to dance.

Now let's try the same thing with a shorter rein.

As you ride, your horse needs the clear direction and support you give him not only through your legs but through your arms and hands as well. Remember the funnel you created with arms, hands and reins in the exercises in Chapter 3? We'll be doing the same thing here.

> **Step 1:** Now pick up the reins and repeat your cycle of Release, Rotate, Connect, Come On, Thank You to check your horse's connection to you. Once you're connected, do it again, only this time add some rotations to the cycle. Release, rotate one or two degrees, then Connect, Come On, Thank You. Your horse should begin to bend in the direction of your rotation.

> **Step 2:** Maintain contact and support with the horse as he bends and finds his balance. It may be necessary to stretch back more on one rein or the other. The amount of stretch depends on the feel of the horse. Is he falling in or out? Do you want to make a smaller or bigger circle? Are you trying to move sideways?

When you rotate your body, and your pelvis is in neutral with a released spine—whether you ride with one hand or both—the horse feels the differentiation of movement between the two sides. Also as you rotate to the inside, it provides more support on the outside rein. All this is supported by more or less rhythm from the legs. The connection lightens as the horse rebalances and the energy of the hind legs comes through his body.

If your horse resists you by falling to the outside, you need to add more stretch on the outside, more rotation to the inside and more ta-daa with the legs. Then say thank you. If your horse is falling in, as you rotate, connect, ta-daa, thank you, you will notice more heaviness on the inside rein. To counteract this, "meet" (as explained under "meet and melt", page 52) longer and release slower on the inside rein.

If he continues to lean on the rein, don't give in to the impulse to brace against the tug by tightening. When a horse is leaning, he's really needing support to get his hind end moving. Any bracing or squeezing by the rider just adds to the horse's imbalance. Remember, when you tighten your spine, your hips automatically lock, making it more difficult for the horse to balance and move. If you keep your spine released, your lower body can be grounded and secure in the saddle. If he still resists, change direction to break his cycle and bring his mind back to you and his confidence back to him. Then try your circle again.

> **Step 3:** Continue to move your horse left, right and around obstacles or "s" shapes. Practice "meet and melt" until you are comfortable with the feel of it. Make sure your horse walks lively. An animated walk keeps his mind on his work and concentrating with you. A slow, dull walk allows him to wander mentally and become distracted. Don't be discouraged if all of this feels awkward at first. So was learning how to tie your shoes the first time. It was a process of learning first one step, then another until finally you could put it all together without even thinking. This is the same thing. We're trying to learn a skill made up of multiple actions. It takes time. Eventually it will become second nature—just like tying a shoe.

Changing Speeds
Now that we have the basic feeling of the walk, let's look at changing speeds in connection.

Step 1: Start off balanced (and rebalance as often as necessary) in a free walk with a loose rein. Both you and your horse should be synchronizing your tempo. Stay at this speed for three or four minutes.

Step 2: When you and your horse are ready, move into a more extended walk. In the more extended walk, the horse should step under more with his hind legs at each stride without quickening his tempo or losing his clear, regular four-beat rhythm. When both of you are in balance, he should reach well forward from the hips and shoulders, and his head and neck should extend forward. His hind feet will overstep well forward of the prints of the front feet. To move into the more extended walk, think forward, rotate your upper body slightly and increase the rhythm of your legs as if you are marching with more intent. Walk "big" steps. Your movement won't look "bigger", it will feel bigger and the horse will take longer strides. Stay at the extended walk for four or five strides.

Step 3: Now think, slow down and walk "small" steps. Move from the more extended walk back into the walk by slowing the rhythm of your body, and think forward. Be careful not to push in the stirrups to slow down. Pushing in the stirrups adds tension to the back and puts the upper body behind the motion. Bring your horse back to the free walk, and continue once more around the arena. Practice changing speeds from less to more to less again until you're comfortable enough to make the transitions smoothly.

Connected Stopping

Most people don't realize it, but stopping takes as much dynamic balance and thought as moving. In the first chapter, our discussion on equine movement related how a horse initiates movement. Movement begins by flexing and swinging the hind leg under, striking the ground, briefly supporting the body and then thrusting back to propel the body forward. All of this movement is transmitted through the horse's spine.

Imagine the horse as a train. If brakes were applied hard at the front of the train, the cars would jam up, each one crashing into the one in front of it. If a horse stops hard on the forehand, his body has a similar reaction. Stopped suddenly, all that forward motion coming from behind reverberates backward and causes a jam-up through the spine. For the horse to stop in balance, the stop has to come from his engine—from behind. This requires two actions on the part of the rider.

The first action is sliding up the rein, lending support to the front end and creating a boundary for the hind end. Place the third and fourth (middle and ring) fingers in between the reins of one hand and slide this hand up to touch the mane line, taking the slack out of the rein with the other hand, and creating a boundary. This movement contains the front end and allows the horse's hind end to come up under him with neutral pelvis. It also overrides the rider's tendency to lean back, tighten the spine and pull on the reins.

The rider should be maintaining movement (resist stiffening) while sliding up the rein. Then, think forward, stretch back and march a little. This helps keep the horse's hind end coming under him. Then the rider should slow the motion of her body to signal the horse to match her motion and slow down. If you've kept your lower back and legs soft and released, you'll be able to sit quietly, stay with the horse's motion, think the stop and then stop walking to achieve the halt. Over time you can omit the step of sliding up.

I know this is contrary to the way many people have been taught to stop a horse, but if you squeeze with your legs, tighten your bottom or back, lean back or push on the stirrups, you're inviting the front of the train to stop and the cars to jam up behind.

Slowing Down The Train

This exercise overrides the tendency riders have to pull on the reins, lean back and tighten their back and seat in a downward transition. It also teaches riders to rotate, connect and march all at the same time. As an added bonus, this exercise also helps to free up the horse's withers and pelvis and allows him to step under. If your horse has a habit of lifting his head and neck or tucking during a transition, this exercise will help override those habits.

Step 1: Prepare to ride by thinking Release, Rotate, Connect, Come On, Thank You. Then move your horse out into a lively, balanced walk. Go once or twice around the arena to get everyone comfortable and connected.

Step 2: Move one hand into the slide-up position (middle and ring finger between the reins). Slide your hand forward to the mane line. Maintain a bend in your elbow and as you touch the mane feel your elbow stretch back in a small isometric flexion. This movement will be invisible, but will be felt by the horse.

Step 3: Maintain motion with your legs, slowing it down as you maintain connection through the shortened reins. As your hand touches the mane, your elbow stretches back and you stop walking.

Step 4: Relax your back and arm muscles to a melt, and slowly slide back on the rein, releasing the front end. Rest for a moment, check your balance and then move your horse back into a lively walk. Practice stopping at a walk until you and your horse do this exercise easily and naturally. Eventually the horse will stop just by your doing Release, Connect, Come On (stop), Thank You.

Back Up

This combination of sliding and ta-daa has other uses as well. The first is backing up.

Step 1: Starting from the halt, slide to the mane and ta-daa your legs. Keep a bend in your elbow, think forward with your upper body, stretch with your elbow and breathe! Your horse will back up.

Step 2: As soon as he softens his neck and releases his poll, slide back slowly on the rein. This is your "Thank You" for his attention and compliance.

Step 3: Repeat the process, backing your horse up first one step, then three steps, then five steps. Melt slowly on the rein each time you get flexion (he dips his chin). This action not only helps the horse learn the valuable skill of backing up when you need him to, it's also a good way to bring his mind back to you. Engage the mind and the body will follow. A note of caution: be careful with a horse that tends to tuck too deep. If he does, ask for fewer steps or intersperse back-up steps with some walking forward. Over time, you can omit the step of sliding up the rein and back up simply with Release, Rotate, Connect, Come On (walk back), Thank You.

Practice this for only a few minutes. A horse is never done training (neither are we), so this basic work should be done routinely. Just remember not to over-drill.

Wake Up

You can also wake up a horse who has started to feel dull or slow by sliding up the rein and adding ta-daa vibrations. This action lets him know you want him to engage and take responsibility for his hind leg power instead of just poking along. It might help to think of this as an exaggerated rebalancing cycle, the slide up functioning like the stretch back and the ta-daa breaking up rigidity. As you slide up, you'll breathe, filling your back. Immediately, as you ta-daa, you'll blow or think forward to the plumb line. At the same time, you will melt, softening your arm and back muscles, saying "Thank you" to the horse. Again, it's Release, Rotate, Connect, Come On, Thank You. By doing this, you'll build lightness and responsiveness in an animal that is not paying attention and almost certainly out of balance.

Step 1: Slide your hand up the rein. Keep your wrist straight and the knuckles of your hand resting against the mane.

Step 2: Stretch your elbow back toward your body, keeping your hand soft. You can take the slack out of the rein with your free hand. If your horse normally tends to be light and fluffy, you can stay in a sitting position as you wake him up. If he's a bit of a slug, you may need more to get his engine going. Leaning forward just enough to take the pressure off your seat bones will let your legs ta-daa in a more powerful way. Also, if your horse is accustomed to over-flexing, do less. Let up on the slide and ta-daa with more oomph.

Step 3: Ta-daa, thinking him forward, light and lively.

Whether you use this combination to wake up a horse or slow him down to a halt, remember that the reason for the ta-daa—for using your legs alternately in a shivery motion—is to break up the tension (which can feel like sluggishness) in the horse's body. Only then can the hind end engage to move the horse forward. The engagement allows the top line to lengthen and the horse to find his own balance so he can carry himself.

Connecting the Trot

Now that we've walked, changed speeds, stopped, backed up and awakened our horses, we can move on to the more energetic action of the trot. The trot is a two-beat diagonal gait with suspension, executed in two time. The diagonal pair of feet strike the ground together for one hoof beat, then the horse pushes off and is suspended in the air for a moment before the opposite diagonal pair of feet strike for the second beat. This action causes the horse to spring the rider and send her up at each stride. This spring creates a shock to the body that the rider feels primarily in the hip, knee, ankle joints and arch of the foot. To help disperse some of the bouncing motion of the trot, most riders learn to post or rise to the trot. You can sit or do a balance position at the trot as well. For our purposes, though, we'll talk about the posting trot.

When a rider posts, or rises to the trot, he moves with one diagonal pair of legs. Usually this is the outside diagonal. The reason is not tradition, but biomechanics. By staying with the outside diagonal, you're springing up as his inside hind is springing forward. This makes it easier for the horse to engage well during a turn. Be sure to change diagonals whenever you change directions. If the body is rigid, staying on one side puts more stress on those legs and can lead to the horse becoming stiffer on a side that is already stiff.

At first you may find it more difficult to stay connected at the trot. But if you've spent enough time at the walk and have built up your body's muscle memory of being in neutral pelvis position, you should be able to find your balance in time. Don't be discouraged if it takes awhile. Remember to rebalance as often as needed by breathing, stretching, applying a ta-daa and blowing out (Release, Rotate, Connect, Come On, Thank You.

Step 1: Prepare yourself for the trot by beginning with the cycle of Release, Rotate, Connect, Come On, Thank You. Move out in a lively walk. After a few strides, repeat the cycle and give him a trot rhythm from your "marching" legs. Remember to let the horse spring you and then you can accentuate or lessen the spring.

Step 2: With your partner watching to help you judge your position, trot around the arena several times. How does it feel?

If you're in balance, you should feel lighter and fluffier. Some riders even say that their legs feel sloppy because they are so used to being compressed. The thighs will also feel looser. That's because, in a relaxed position, you're not tightening up your back and locking your hinges. Let it happen. Enjoy the freedom.

Step 3: Slow from a trot to a walk by sliding up on the reins, thinking about posting slower. As you move into a sitting position, keep your knees and your back soft and springy. Think forward. Let your thighs feel like inner tubes that are buoyant and riding the waves of the ocean. Rebalance as needed. Remember, soften when you feel the urge to push down on the stirrups. If you're still working on overriding old habits of stiffening and pulling, you'll have to be conscious of letting go in different areas of your body.

Once you're trotting in connection well, you can work on riding shallow loops, or "S's" at the walk and trot. Always strive to maintain connection with the horse's mouth through the elbows and rebalance often.

Less Is More

Once people feel the connection with the horse and then lose it again (we all do and often), the natural tendency is to push to get it back. This is the time to think, "Let go, release." If you become frustrated, remember your mind may be getting in the way more than your body. Take a minute to just sit there, put your knees up on the pommel, tune into your breathing and buoy. After a few minutes you may be able to go on. If not, just stop. These frustrating times are not failures—they're stepping stones. Just relax and accept the value of where you are at the moment. You are in the process of releasing old patterns

As you establish a routine for working with *Connected Riding*®, strive for small successes. When you achieve them, quit for the day—even if it's only 15 minutes into your session. If you drill your horse over and over again until you're both dead tired, neither one of you will look forward to your next session together.

When you've had a successful session, remember to show yourself and your horse some appreciation—a hug or a nice neck rub for him and maybe a relaxing bath or a few chapters of a good book for you—anything that reminds both of you that life is better when it's lived without stress.

I know it takes thought and will to overcome old habits and establish newer, healthier ones. But the rewards are so great. Just take your time. There's no timetable for success. By allowing both you and your horse to progress at a comfortable pace, you'll have a much greater chance of forming a rewarding partnership that lasts.

Chapter 6

Translations

*"The farther off from England, the nearer
is to France, so turn not pale, beloved snail,
but come and join the dance."*

Lewis Carroll

If you've been around horses as long as I have, you know there are many ways to learn riding. Most of you probably started by taking lessons at a local barn. If you later became interested in competition, you probably progressed to a trainer in a particular discipline or breed. Then, of course, there were clinics, visiting instructors and training tips from friends. And now there's this book! All in all, I'll bet most of you have put in enough hours of instruction to earn a college degree.

This, in and of itself, isn't a bad thing. We should never stop learning. The problem I encountered over the years was trying to translate the teachings of one instructor into the language of another. Everyone seemed to have her own way of asking for a particular result. It was very confusing. To add to the confusion, few instructors actually told me how to get a result or even why they were asking for it. I just did what I was told and hoped for the best. When the instructor was with me, it usually worked out. The problem came when I was on my own.

Because I had learned by rote instruction, instead of feel, I didn't truly understand what was "correct". But, as I began developing the understanding that led to *Connected Riding*®, I started to feel, more than hear, what they were asking. Finally, when someone said "more leg" I knew what they meant—and I knew what to do. You can imagine my relief. I didn't have to waste the time, money and effort I'd put into learning how to ride over the past 30 years. I just had to find a way to translate that learning from a language of concepts into a language of feelings. And I did.

What follows are some of those translations. It's my hope that they will help you honor the instruction you've had over the years and incorporate into your future instruction a new way of learning by feeling and understanding.

Sit Up Straight

This is probably one of the most common commands in riding instruction.

Purpose:	To place the body in an erect position.
Correction:	Usually the rider is hunched over (Pocket Sitter) or hollow-backed (Arched Equitator and Gumby).
Traditional Instruction:	Pull the shoulders back and lift the chest up.
Connected® **Translation:**	Place the pelvis in the neutral position, find your buoy and breathe.

Comments: When instructors give this command, they are usually trying to correct a postural habit of the rider. For a short while, the traditional instruction will probably work. The Pocket Sitter who hunches forward will temporarily appear to be more erect when she pulls her shoulders back and lifts her chest. However, in reality, she's just trading one postural dysfunction for another and won't be able to maintain it. If she adjusted her pelvis to the neutral position, her body would fall into an erect posture naturally. Rebalancing would keep her position erect and the instructor happy.

The same is true of the Arched Equitator or the Gumby®. This rider is usually leaning forward because she's so tight in the pelvis that her upper body is pulled forward. Trying to bring her body back in alignment by exaggerating the hollow in her back that is already present will do nothing more than further tighten her back and pelvis. It will be impossible for her to maintain this position for long without experiencing pain. Again, this rider needs to adjust the position of her pelvis to allow the body to fall into a naturally erect posture.

I received positive proof that this works when I was asked to teach two young riders with Cerebral Palsy. Everyone, including myself, thought the young people were unable to keep their bodies erect because of the debilitating effects of their disease. Despite their condition, I decided to apply the same *Connected Riding*® principles to them that I used with all my students. I wasn't all that surprised when they became erect after I helped them move their pelvises into neutral position. It usually works for everyone. The real surprise came in the length of time they were able to maintain that erectness. For a full half hour, these students rode upright in the saddle. They had never been able to do that before. It was a special day for all of us.

So the next time your instructor tells you to sit up straight, just smile and adjust your pelvis into the neutral position and "think forward". If you rebalance as needed, chances are you won't have to hear that command again for awhile.

Sit Back

This command is common in most disciplines and is used primarily when working on downward transitions.

Purpose:	To keep the upper body in alignment during downward transitions.
Correction:	The upper body is tipping forward.
Traditional Instruction:	Push the upper body back, placing pressure in the stirrup.
Connected® Translation:	Rebalance the body, keeping all hinges free.

Comments: Once you've allowed your body to tip forward, you have to work very hard to push yourself back through the force of the transition to correct your position. Because this is difficult, most riders end up jamming the system of both the horse and rider. All rider types are prone to tipping forward—the Arched Equitator and Gumby® because of their tight pelvises and spines and the Pocket Sitter because of his collapsed sternum. However, if you're in a connected position, your body will be able to right itself naturally as it moves with the force of the transition.

Shoulders Back

This command is an excellent example of a problem that is caused by postural habits that make it almost impossible to ride in a way the instructor is expecting.

Purpose:	To achieve balance for both rider and horse.
Correction:	Shoulders are pulled forward and/or the horse is hanging on the rider.
Traditional Instruction:	Pull your shoulders back.
Connected® Translation:	Adjust pelvis to neutral position and think lightness in the hands and wrists. Find your buoy and do the "bubble gum" exercise.

Comments: As you might guess, this is something that the Pocket Sitter hears all the time because of his habitual collapsed posture. But she's not alone. The Arched Equitator and the Gumby are also candidates for the "shoulders back" command because their arched backs bring chins and therefore shoulders forward.

Unfortunately, it's unlikely that these riders are asked for a "shoulders back" correction because of a momentary lapse in posture. It's more likely that they have habitual problems that can't be corrected simply by a command. They need to change postural habits in order to maintain the erect position for which the instructor is asking. So if you're hearing "shoulders back" often, you need to begin by recognizing your postural challenges and work toward changing them.

Facing this challenge will do more than eliminate an annoying command from your instructor. It will also help you and your horse function better together. Often when you pull your shoulders forward, your horse will "hang" on you. Here's what usually happens: When you feel the hang of the horse, you tense your wrists, push your hands down and curl your shoulders forward. This puts a huge amount of pressure on your arms, your hands are pulling away, you're stressing your pectoral muscles and your shoulders keep curling. This not only creates a lot of work, it reinforces the incorrect shoulder position.

Since you already came to the horse with poor riding posture, maybe from your work or old habits, prolonged riding in this position can lead to muscle atrophy in some places and overdevelopment in others. In extreme cases, the points of the shoulders are actually pulled forward by the overexertion of the muscles in an incorrect way over a long period of time. The only way this can be released is by awareness (you stop doing it) and having bodywork done that releases some of the adhesions that have formed in the upper body.

What I find unfortunate is that so many commands, including "shoulders back," are mechanical and drill a position into your brain that your body often has difficulty performing. So riders often feel like they're not very good learners; they're always doing something wrong; or they're not very successful, at least not until they have a breakthrough.

Or they think it's a breakthrough. Often these "breakthroughs" come because an instructor says you need to be put on the lunge line. As a good student, you work really, really hard at achieving a position and you do it and do it and do it until finally you reach total exhaustion and the body lets go. That's when the instructor says, "There, that's it!" You think you got it because of all your hard work, when, in essence, you got it because you were so exhausted your body released and settled into a position of natural balance. Believe me, it's much easier to get some good bodywork and then ride in a connected position. Think about it.

Heels Down

This is something beginning riders and hunt seat riders hear often.

Purpose:	To provide security for the rider.
Correction:	With beginners it often corrects heels up.
Traditional Instruction:	Push your heels down.
Connected® Translation:	Place the stirrup behind the ball of the foot and keep all hinges free and soften the upper thigh muscles.

Comments: We're really dealing with two different types of riders with the "heels down" command. First, we'll talk about the beginning rider. Many beginning riders are insecure, so they tend to cling with their thighs in an attempt to hold on. This tightens their backs and causes their heels to pull up. So it's natural for an instructor to ask them to put their heels down. To give the new rider the most secure position in the stirrups, however, the instructors should be telling the students to make their foot parallel to the ground with the stirrup behind the ball of the foot. I realize this is a bit controversial. I've had many instructors question me about this.

But a level foot isn't something I've invented. Look under the hunter division in the AHSA rule book. The picture in the book shows a level foot. Once instructors try this position they never question it again. Why? Because in this position, all the hinges of the lower body work and can absorb the movement of the horse. The rider remains springy, able to respond and very secure. So it's important for beginning riders to use this position for the most secure ride.

Next we'll look at the hunt seat rider. "Heels down" is almost an everyday mantra for the hunter world, and I've seen people work very hard to achieve this position. But when they push their heels down, they jam the leg into a fixed position. This gives them a false sense of security. And basically it's like being put into a "James Bond" ejection seat. If a horse stops dead in front of a jump, the rider has a much better chance of ejecting out of the saddle because there's no spring left in the body to absorb the shock. Not a good thing.

Also, in such activities as working over fences, the two-point position asks the rider to get his seat up out of the saddle. This asks the rider to work while half standing. This position tenses his knees as well as the rest of the leg, because the rider is half gripping all the time. I prefer what I call a "modified" two-point position that allows the rider to move his upper body forward by closing the angle of the pelvis. This position still maintains the plumb line of ear, shoulder, hip, ankle without having to stand out of the saddle. It also allows the rider to ask the horse to "come on" or "ta-daa" with as much vigor as needed while still maintaining a secure seat.

Finally, it's very common for a rider approaching a fence to think, "Get your chest up, hollow your back and get your heels down." Unfortunately this doesn't put the rider in a secure position either, and it tends to put the horse on the forehand. If the horse is on the forehand and really avoiding, you have to increase what you're doing. This method has you pushing your heels down more, arching your back more, pulling more on the reins and squeezing more with your legs. It's an incredible cycle of hard work that's very difficult to change and isn't as effective. Hunt seat people who've applied *Connected Riding*® techniques have found much of the hard work is lessened when they stop shoving their heels down, thus avoiding jamming up the horse and their own body. They also report feeling more secure. Those who've been riding for a long time admit it is a hard habit to break. But eventually they did, and they're glad they stuck with it. In time, their horses jumped better, landed better and stopped better.

Forward Movement Commands

Commands asking for forward movement such as "push him forward," "liven him up" or even "close your leg" are used by almost every trainer at one time or another.

Purpose:	Produce active forward movement to maintain forward motion.
Correction:	The horse is dull or looking "disconnected".

Traditional Instruction:	Squeeze your legs and push with your seat.
Connected® Translation:	Release, Rotate, Connect, Come On, Thank You.

Comments: These commands are often used when a horse has lost his focus, becomes dull or is resistant to a rider's effort to move forward. Unfortunately, most riders follow these instructions by squeezing their legs or pushing with their seats, which jams the hips and makes them dead weight on the back of the horse. Remember, horses' bellies move from side to side. So when you clamp down with both legs you can't follow their natural rhythm of left/right, causing compression in both the horse and rider. This in turn disables the horse's ability to do what you're asking by restricting his freedom of movement. You might temporarily "wake" him up by squeezing, but you won't really achieve true forward motion.

In addition to compression, if you aren't following the left/right motion of the horse, you'll probably put him on the forehand. This prevents his back from coming up and jams up his motion. We have to remember that we're not riding kangaroos or jackrabbits. Our legs need to function in an alternating fashion, just like the horse. Then we'll stay with the motion.

So, when an instructor asks you for more forward activity, it's time to get back to basics. Move your pelvis into neutral, breathe, rotate slightly, connect with your horse through the reins, tell him to come on with the alternating motion of ta-daa and then slowly release the reins back to the original pressure, and say "Thank you" for his efforts. At first you might find this difficult to do while in motion. And you'll be trying to overcome the habit of squeezing, which also takes time. But with practice you'll become comfortable with the "connected" way of encouraging forward movement. Once that happens, it can be done as often as needed to keep your horse moving forward and attentive.

Frame Commands

Another set of common commands are those given to affect the frame of the horse. These might include "Go round" or "Collect him up."

Purpose:	To put the horse in a proper frame.
Correction:	Horse is not in the correct frame needed for proper execution of a movement.
Traditional Instruction:	"Go round," Collect him up," Get your horse underneath you," or "Put him on the bit."
***Connected®* Translation:**	Release, Rotate, Connect, Come On, Thank You. (You will use more or less rotation of the upper body depending on gait, exercise being executed and physical condition of the horse.)

Comments: To address these commands we have to go back to basic biomechanical understanding of the movement of the horse. For a horse to round his body, he must release his poll, come up through the withers and bring his hind end underneath himself. Many riders try to achieve this just by shortening the reins or wagging the horse's head back and forth. This will signal the horse that you want him to pull himself into a rounded frame, but if he is restricted by you, his own body, or equipment and devices, the frame he achieves will be artificial and difficult to maintain.

This is probably the result that most of you have been getting. I have rarely seen a truly collected horse—even at the highest levels of dressage. Why? Because usually horse, rider or both are jammed somewhere. But don't be discouraged. Through releasing your body you will reach ultimate collection. Here's how:

Begin by evaluating your horse and the equipment you use on him. Is your horse capable of the kind of collection you're looking for? I've met many horses who were physically incapable of performing a certain job because of physical considerations or problems with equipment. If a horse's teeth are unbalanced or have sharp points, it's difficult and painful for him to release his poll. The balance of the feet should also be considered. A long toe or a low heel will jam the body. And if a saddle is jamming a horse, he can't possibly go round. In some workshops all I've done is change the saddle on a horse and suddenly the horse has gone round—sometimes for the first time. The owners were amazed. All the hard work they had been going through could have been saved with a new saddle.

A horse's angles also need to be evaluated. Does he have a long or short back, a long or short neck? Is his forearm long or short? Some types of conformation are better suited to do some of the things we ask. Not every horse is a good candidate for high collection. Review your horse's conformation and only ask of him what he's capable of doing. You also need to make sure he's not physically jammed up as well. If he is, begin by doing groundwork exercises to help him loosen up. Finally, apply the *Connected Riding®* methods.

Kick Him On or More Leg

This is something riders hear from instructors and learn on their own by watching other riders.

Purpose:	To achieve greater impulsion.
Correction:	To speed up a horse that is bogging down.
Traditional Instruction:	Kick the horse repeatedly to get him moving or keep him moving or squeeze with more intensity.
Connected® Translation:	Place your pelvis in the neutral position, breathe and come-on with vigorous ta-daas. Make sure your legs are working in an alternating motion. Ride the rhythm.

Comments: Whenever a horse starts dying on you, someone is going to tell you to kick him on. This may be because you're making a run for the win after clearing the last barrel, or maybe you don't want your horse to bog down or stop on you in front of a fence. But whatever the reason, I have to say that kicking a horse on is one of the most useless acts we can commit during riding.

Some of you might take exception to that statement. I don't

make it to upset anyone or to make anyone feel badly about what they've been doing with their horse. I say it because, biomechanically, it has no real impact on encouraging greater impulsion.

"But it works," people have said to me. Yes, if a horse knows that when he hears that whap, whap, whap sound caused by both of your legs slapping against his sides, he's supposed to get a move on, he will. But that's just a mechanical aid. The sound is what's getting him moving—not the action. In fact, the action is actually restricting him from giving you the full impulsion you want.

Remember the frog on the ball? When we use our legs in an alternating motion we not only stay with the motion of the horse, we can communicate our desire for motion to the horse. And we allow him the freedom to give us that motion. So instead of kicking a horse on or squeezing harder—ta-daa him on. When you fast-forward your rhythm with this alternating motion and your back is released, you'll be surprised at the power he'll give you when you need it most. Do it for 2 or 3 strides, see what happens and then repeat until you achieve the desired impulsion. The maintenance will take less effort.

Half Halt

Volumes have been written on the half halt. While the term is used primarily in English riding, other disciplines also use the same concept.

Purpose:	To ask for more attention and action with increased collection and lightness, without restriction or loss of rhythm.
Correction:	The horse is inattentive or needs to be more alert and instantly responsive.
Traditional Instruction:	Apply a brief and positive outside rein aid coordinated with a strong, mainly inside, leg aid. You might also hear, "Close both hands, sit deep, close the leg and sit up."
Connected® Translation:	Float the upper body to the forward part

of the buoy. Then Rotate, Connect, Come
On with the legs, allowing the calves to
provide a light "lift" to the belly of the
horse, and then Thank You.

Comments: The half halt is an instantaneous "wake up" call to prepare
an inattentive horse physically and mentally for the execution of a
movement, or a signal that something is about to change to the attentive horse. Physically, we want him to improve his balance through a
brief moment of increased releasing of the poll, bringing up the withers and back, and bringing the hind end under. Mentally, we're asking him to pay attention—or get ready for the movement. It should
be executed in a very brief, one-step action without restriction or loss
of rhythm. When it's correctly applied, the half halt should lead to
lightness in the rein contact and self-carriage in the horse.

That's the ideal. Unfortunately, the ideal is usually not achieved
because the methods we use to perform the half halt—driving with
the seat, bringing the upper body back, closing the legs, and pulling
with the hands—tends to provoke contraction in the horse's back.
This tightness makes it difficult to achieve the lightness and
throughness that the half halt should produce. Often the horse will
hesitate when you drive him and pull on him, but he doesn't
achieve the true desired result.

Instead of performing compressive actions, we should be helping
the horse to rebalance—that is, release the poll, bring up the withers,
and bring under the hind end. This will add lightness and bring the
weight from the forehand to the hind end, where the power is locat-
ed. When this happens, horse and rider have access to increased power.

To execute a truly effective half halt, you need to float the upper
body forward to the foremost part of the buoy. This movement
allows you to maintain connection through the force of the horse's
motion and automatically places the direction of the elbow back. As
the upper body is going forward (this movement is minute and the
upper body does not appear to go ahead of the vertical) and the
elbow is coming back, the lower back stays free and open, which

invites the upper leg of the rider to be round to receive the back of the horse coming up. As the thighs of the rider are brought up with the motion of the stride, the calf automatically "comes on", giving a little lift to the belly of the horse at the same instant. This actually helps to lift the back of the horse so the hind leg can come under. It sounds like a lot, but it only takes an instant and it achieves all the desired results you and your instructor want.

Final Notes
As you have probably figured out by now, the underlying recipe for most commands is to:
- Place the pelvis in neutral position—readjusting seat if necessary.
- Find your buoy and float forward.
- Rotate the upper body.
- Connect through the reins in an elastic way so that you're ready to add more or less connection depending on what the horse needs.
- Acknowledge the marching rhythm with your body.
- Ride the rhythm of the horse.
- Say Thank You.

All of this can be done through softness, lightness and adding motion in your body or changing the motion when you need to. It is a beautiful, easy, connected way to ride. And it creates a lasting partnership with your horse.

As you continue on your path of learning with your horse, you will be able to use what you've discovered here to make your riding more productive and enjoyable for you and your horse. There are many avenues open to you. I know if you look closely, you'll see that everyone who takes the welfare of the horse to heart and appreciates the beauty in the partnership of the dance, is looking for the same thing. Sometimes riders just ask for it in different ways.

Just remember: The only constant is change, the only freedom is movement.

Quick Reference Glossary

Allow: Allowing time for horse to respond to request from rider; to find its balance in the execution of the movement being asked. Also softening of muscles in riders' body to "allow" movement.

Clear funnel: A supportive, directive connection that creates a clear path for horse to move through. Accomplished by keeping the outside rein on the side of the neck, close to the mane line, searchlight turned in direction of turn, back full and released, elbows elastic and connected to the bit. The inside rein allows the horse to come through by being off the neck. The reins never cross the mane line.

Come on, come on/Bump-up/Pick up the hind end/Fluff the belly: The first stage of collection. With rider's back released, a good connection through the reins, rotation of upper body, increased connection and support by backward stretch of elbows while doing ta-daa actively with the legs. This is asking the horse to come from behind into a supporting rein and then slowly releasing and allowing him to come under to self-carriage. The horse releases the poll, softens the neck, brings up its base (lifts the withers), rounds its spine and brings its hind end under. In the beginning stages, it is an obvious movement often requiring the rider to slide up a bit on the reins to find the horse's connecting place. If a horse is stiff, however, he will start by raising his head. Eventually, the horse will learn to release his hind end and the head will lower.

Connected Riding®: A biomechanical system of riding that enables rider and horse to synchronize through movement. The rider is a metronome that sets the rhythm and direction of the dance, influencing the horse's movements through an elastic connection rather than pressure or compression. Through a supportive body dynamic, a cycle of movement passes from the horse through the rider's body, returning through the horse in a synchronized, reciprocal, rhythmical manner. This system of riding encompasses all disciplines without the use of artificial aids and supports the fullest potential of every horse and rider.

Connection: Contact. A supportive and elastic point of contact on the reins that allows the horse and rider to feel each other, bit to elbow. Also, the synergy of movement of horse and rider.

Equitation: The proper balance and position that allows maximum freedom of motion for both horse and rider (regardless of task at hand)—creating, supporting and allowing self-carriage.

"Float": Allowing rider's body to rebalance to "noon" position on the clock or plumb line by following their exhaling breath forward and out of the mouth. This enables the rider's lower back to soften and widen, and the spine to expand and lengthen, thus taking pressure off the hips, and allowing them to move independently.

Frog on a ball: Rider's legs "surround" horse's belly as a frog on a ball. It feels as if the knees minutely bend and lift to allow rider's calf to find the belly of the horse. This allows freedom of movement of rider's legs to march, or ta-daa, or fluff independently of each other. Legs appear to be wrapped onto the horse but are not because they are soft, light and movable. If a rider just bends the knee and places their lower leg on the horse without that minute lift of their knee, the legs will become tightly wrapped on the horse, the hips will lock, the legs will be unable to move independently and the lower leg will grip.

Grounded feet: Feeling the weight of the leg as it is supported by the stirrup without pushing down in the stirrups. Imagine if the horse were to disappear from under the rider, the rider would land with both feet flat on the ground falling neither forward nor backward.

Mane line: Crest of horse's neck; point of connection when "sliding up" to stop, slow, back up or hook an index finger for stability. The hands do not cross over the mane line.

Marching rhythm of legs: Following horse's rhythm as the rider's legs surround the horse's belly. If the horse slows down, rider has responsibility to accentuate "marching" rhythm, increasing the tempo so the horse catches up. If the horse speeds up then the rider can slow the rhythm of the march. The movement is imperceptible.

Meet and Melt: The rider meets the connection (matches the pressure) the horse gives on the reins, and then very slowly softens the muscles in their back, rib cage and arms without moving the arms. This allows the horse to find his balance without needing to be rigid or held up. When very refined, "meet" is an inhalation felt through the reins and "melt" an exhalation, giving the horse a subtle rhythm to elasticize with and reciprocate. When the horse is in balance and released through the spine, the "meet and melt" becomes a part of the reciprocal dance of rhythm and rebalancing that is a subconscious sharing of true partnership. Can be in a rhythm of long stretch, slow give or short stretch, slow give.

Noon: Rider's point of true balance in the saddle on the plumb line: ear, shoulder, hip and ankle. The lower back is released and soft, allowing the upper body to move freely from the hip joints and the lower body to feel grounded and centered.

Outside rein to the mane line: Outside hand comes to the mane line as the horse needs support.

Releasing the base: Movement of horse during which the muscles of the neck, shoulders, withers and rib cage soften, neck elongates and back can move upwards. Poll lowers, withers lift, hind end comes under.

Release, rotate, connect, come on, thank you: The process of rebalancing when needed, as in preparation for a transition or lateral movement.

Release/soften the back: Filling the lower back by taking an inhaling breath "up the spine," filling the lower back first and breathing out as if to blow out a candle. This is accomplished when inhaling by allowing the diaphragm to expand, the muscles of the lumbar area relax, which feels as if the lower back "fills." (This is instead of taking a shallow breath that pulls the chest upward and hollows the lumbar area.)

Ride the rhythm/march: Proactively follow or accentuate rhythm of the horse's motion. The rider is the metronome.

Rotate: Use of searchlight.

Searchlight: Imaginary beacon of light shining out from the sternum to the belly button; used to position rider's upper body for transitions, turning, bending, straightness and lateral movements. The upper body rotates on a plane parallel to the ground—does not twist or collapse in turning. The muscles in the rib cage and back stay soft.

Self-carriage: When a horse comes through and the rider feels the energy of the hind feet pushing the horse forward. The horse's base is up, back is up and under the rider, the horse's head is vertical or slightly ahead of the vertical. The horse feels energetic, light, supple and free. The poll and withers are released and the hindquarters engaged. Minor rebalancing maintains the feeling of power and elasticity.

Sliding up the reins: Rein length shortens by placing third and fourth (middle and ring) fingers of one hand in between the reins and sliding up toward or to the mane line for more support and connection, taking the slack out of the rein with the other hand. It gives the horse a clear boundary so the front end is contained and the hind end can activate and "catch up" to the front end. Once the hind end is activated, sliding up is rarely necessary. Sliding up is used to teach a horse to step up with his hind legs into the halt and to override a rider's habit of leaning back and pulling on the reins.

Stretchy, elastic elbows: The soft and elastic connection of a rider's elbows to the bit. The rider "meets" the connection with the bit and "melts" slowly to allow the horse to rebalance and maintain connection. The rider's back must be soft to avoid a pulling motion or "riding from the hands". The movement is felt in the arms and follows the horse's head. A locomotive action of forward down then back and up is achieved with a feeling of lightness in the forearm.

Ta-daa/Come On: A light, shivery, alternating leg motion done with a released back that induces the horse to movement. It can be done more actively as a wake-up call or almost imperceptibly as a soothing reassurance from the rider's legs to the horse's barrel.

Thank You: The slow release, "melting" on the reins. Allows the horse time to respond and the rider time to observe and feel whether horse is coming through or not.

Think forward, march: Reminder to float, and move legs in rhythm with the horse to override the tendency to sit up, freeze, squeeze with the legs and brace in the stirrups, especially when horse moves suddenly.

For further information please contact:

Peggy Cummings
C/O Connected Riding® Clinics
36577 Pico Street
Springfield, OR 97478
1-800-310-2192

www.peggycummings.com